Key Concepts in
Anti-discriminatory
Social Work

The SAGE Key Concepts series provides students with accessible and authoritative knowledge of the essential topics in a variety of disciplines. Cross-referenced throughout, the format encourages critical evaluation through understanding. Written by experienced and respected academics, the books are indispensable study aids and guides to comprehension.

TOYIN OKITIKPI and CATHY AYMER

Key Concepts in
Anti-discriminatory
Social Work

Los Angeles | London | New Delhi
Singapore | Washington DC

SAGE Publications Ltd
1 Oliver's Yard
55 City Road
London EC1Y 1SP

SAGE Publications Inc.
2455 Teller Road
Thousand Oaks, California 91320

SAGE Publications India Pvt Ltd
B 1/I 1 Mohan Cooperative Industrial Area
Mathura Road
New Delhi 110 044

SAGE Publications Asia-Pacific Pte Ltd
33 Pekin Street #02-01
Far East Square
Singapore 048763

Library of Congress Control Number: 2009929641

British Library Cataloguing in Publication data

A catalogue record for this book is available from the
British Library

ISBN 978-1-4129-3081-9
ISBN 978-1-4129-3082-6 (pbk)

Typeset by C&M Digitals (P) Ltd, Chennai, India
Printed by CPI Antony Rowe, Chippenham, Wiltshire
Printed on paper from sustainable resources

Mixed Sources
Product group from well-managed
forests and other controlled sources
www.fsc.org Cert no. SGS-COC-2953
© 1996 Forest Stewardship Council
FSC

The difficulty lies not so much in developing new ideas as in escaping from the old ones. (John Maynard Keynes)

contents

contents

contents

key concepts in anti-discriminatory social work

about the authors

Professor Toyin Okitikpi (FRSA) is a visiting professor at the University of Bedfordshire. He is a lay member on a number of tribunals including: the General Medical Council's Fitness to Practice Panel; the Asylum and Immigration Tribunal, Nursing and Midwifery Interim Order Panel and the Mental Health Review Tribunal. He is also a member of Aventure (a social welfare consultancy group). His social work background is in work with children and families. His research interests include social work education; the importance of education in the lives of children and young people; refugee and asylum-seeking children and their families; social integration and cohesion; working with children of mixed parentage; and interracial/multicultural families and their experiences.

Dr Cathy Aymer is a social work academic, working as a Senior Lecturer in social work in the School of Health Sciences and Social Care at Brunel University and the Director for the Centre for Black Professional Practice. Her social work background is with children and families. Her research interests are black students in higher education and black professionals in welfare organisations; professional responses to refugees and asylum seekers; social work teaching and learning; anti-discriminatory practice in social welfare; the experiences of young black men and professional responses to them; and diversity in organisations. She has published work in these areas.

acknowledgements

This book was inspired by encounters with social welfare practitioners, academics, teachers, health professionals and students from different disciplines. In different ways, they and we have, for many years, been grappling with the complexities of integrating anti-discriminatory ideas into our day-to-day practice. We would like to say a special thank you to Zoe Elliott-Fawcett without whom the book would never have seen the light of day. Many thanks to Dr A.S. Gandy for her help in editing the manuscript. Also a special thank you to Anna Luker, Alice Oven, Susannah Trefgarne and Emma Paterson for their incredible patience. Finally, thank you to Debra Okitikpi for helping with the editing and to Professor John Pitts and Professor Michael Preston-Shoot for their supportive interest in the project.

Introduction

Treating people with kindness, tackling unfairness, and looking for ways to provide appropriate and non-discriminatory practice has a long history in social work (Forsythe 1995). Yet despite the lucidity of the notion, anti-discriminatory practice (ADP) is not necessarily a concept that can be easily integrated into day-to-day practice. Often cited as good practice and a good way of working with people, anti-discriminatory practice is generally presented, rightly, as an approach that is conducive to a positive outcome (Dominelli 2004; Payne 2005; Thompson 2005). Although we agree with the underlying assertions of Payne, Thompson, Dominelli and others, we nevertheless maintain that while it is not impossible for practitioners to adopt anti-discriminatory practice, their ability to embed the approach in their day-to-day practice would be less difficult if their organisation make the necessary changes that support anti-discriminatory practice. In our view, by creating a conducive environment for anti-discriminatory practice to thrive, the organisation would be helping practitioners' self-reflection and facilitating fundamental shift in their attitude and general outlook towards others. There is some evidence of tacit acceptance about the difficulty of implementing anti-discriminatory practice. For example, it is clear that approaches towards anti-discriminatory practice have changed over the years. In its earlier form, there were attempts to change people's beliefs and attitudes, but now there is a move away from individualising and focusing on self-awareness towards greater emphasis on developing legal framework, structures, systems and processes to curb practitioners' discriminatory practices.

A CALL FOR CHANGE

Anti-discriminatory practice was developed in response to social work practices that perpetuated discrimination, injustices and inequalities. The calls for an end to oppression and discrimination have a long history which gained some momentum in the 1960s. However, it was not until the 1970s and 1980s that the demands for equality were formulated into an approach that practitioners could attempt to integrate into their work. Anti-discriminatory practice challenged the negative assumptions that were endemic in society regarding race, social class, gender, age, disability and sexual orientation. During the 1970s and 1980s, there were great concerns among social work practitioners, community groups and political activists (and many other concerned individuals), about the relatively high numbers of black children in the care system. There was also disquiet about the neglect and poor education attainment of both black children and white working-class children; concerns were expressed about society's negative attitudes towards migrants; there was anger about the police's poor response to domestic violence and their racism; the disproportionate numbers of young black men in mental institutions; the criminalisation of non-heterosexual relationships; and the inhuman and degrading provision for people with impairment/ disability. In essence, the call for change and a different response to recipients of social welfare and social work services came from a diverse group of people and organisations.

This book does not make any bold claims or challenge the existing knowledge base of anti-discriminatory practice. Rather, it encourages a revisiting of the concept and an acknowledgement that the driving and fundamental principles of anti-discriminatory practice still holds as good today as when it was first developed. Although in this publication we suggest that anti-discriminatory practice roots were forged during the political hothouse of the 1960s and 1970s, we are in fact reminded by Forsythe (1995) that 'there was clearly a rich tradition of anti-discriminatory theory and practice in nineteenth-century social work, a vision of social inclusion and systematic challenge, within the contexts available, of structures which undermined this' (1995: 14).
He also highlighted, and it is worth quoting in full that:

> There were therefore several traditions in respect of anti-discriminatory in early British social work. On the one hand were groups supporting blatant discriminatory, segregative practices on the basis of Malthusian and neo-Darwinian eugenic theory. On the other hand were the practice and vision of such pioneers as Elizabeth Fry, Samuel Barnett or Josephine Butler which revealed as much more universalist inclusive tradition and sustained, purposeful challenge to structures of discrimination. (Forsythe 1995: 15)

Forsythe further observed that:

> A third group acted in the same way towards their particular group such as Barnardo and yet reinforced, say, the religious discrimination embedded in their social and intellectual context. Fourthly there were many who simply tried to avoid inflicting discrimination on their care group by simple sensitivity and kindness rather than systematic challenge of structures. (1995: 15)

The tradition of sensitivity, kindness, the avoidance of inflicting discrimination and trying to provide a universalist approach has a long history in social work. Of course, it is always the case that each generation is prone to believing that they had the idea first and that they are the ones at the forefront of 'innovative' practice. However, as Forsythe demonstrates, social work has always taken the idea of anti-discrimination practice seriously and has strived from its inception to ensure that the concept is not forgotten and is a core aspect of practice. Anti-discriminatory practice is part of the ethos contained in the health and social care field that supports practice that is grounded within an ethical framework and is guided by the duties, principles and responsibilities as set out in the professions' Code of Practice.

ABOUT THIS BOOK

This book is particularly aimed at practitioners, academics, students, lay readers and service users (since they are now involved in training practitioners and are contributing their knowledge in different areas of service provision). The aim of the book is not to upset people by being unnecessarily provocative. Anti-discriminatory practice, although a good practice, does have the ability to evoke fear, anxiety and mistrust. In some cases, just the mere mention of the concept generally provokes uncomfortable feelings and concerns about being unfairly labelled. Unfortunately, it is not uncommon for discussions and sessions on Anti-discriminatory practice to turn into acrimonious battle grounds with a polarisation of views and intolerant stance being taken by participants. As we know from our own experiences of running training courses, many practitioners have been bruised by their encounters with people who hold discriminatory views and who fail to see what the fuss was all about. Similarly, there are those who feel they are unable to take part in serious exchanges of views about anti-discriminatory practice because they are too afraid of being labelled racists, disabilist, sexists and/or homophobic. One of the overriding objectives of this publication is to encourage discussion to take place and a plea for tolerance and better understanding about differences. It asks for people to be honest and sensitive about the subject and also to acknowledge that this is indeed a difficult subject area to explore. It is important to admit from the outset that no one is perfect and that while a person may experience discrimination and be oppressed by others, they may also, at the same time, discriminate and be oppressive towards other people. In other words, no one person or group has a monopoly on experiencing or perpetuating discrimination or oppression.

This book is divided into two parts. **Part one**, consisting of five chapters, focuses on discussing the concept and the different models of discrimination and the legal framework within which it operates. Chapter 1 explores the nature and the extent of discrimination. It discusses the fact that discrimination has physical, psychological and emotional manifestations. In essence, understanding the nature and impact of discrimination assists in placing anti-discrimination practice in context. Chapter 2 considers different concepts and socio-cultural ideas that underpin discussions about anti-discriminatory practice. It highlights some of the complex dynamics that anti-discriminatory practice has to work within. It also tries to make the point that although the approach is empowering, there is a growing danger of it becoming hijacked by intolerance, oppressive and discriminatory attitudes and beliefs. Chapter 3 demonstrates that there is a tension between approaches that are service-led and those which are service-user focused. It discusses how some organisations straddle between the different camps while others, for good reasons, adopt what is akin to a service-user bias. Chapter 4 explores the political dimension of anti-discriminatory practice. It argues that Anti-discriminatory practice was borne out of political struggles of the 1960s and 1980s. It suggests that while it is understandable that an association could be made between cultural and sexual politics and anti-discriminatory practice, it is just as important to retain the political edge of anti-discriminatory practice. Chapter 5 is interested in exploring the legislative framework that underpins the ideas and philosophy of anti-discriminatory practice. As well as providing an historical overview of how legislation has evolved in this area, it also illustrates the difference between what is actually sanctioned by law and what has developed, increasingly, as a matter of 'culture' within practice. **Part two**, which also consists of five chapters is more practice orientated. Chapter 6 concentrates on the reasons why practitioners would still need to work with anti-discriminatory practice. It argues that, despite the increasing reliance on litigation, the first port of call of discrimination is still the contact and interaction between people. In this context, it is the encounter between the practitioner and the service user that is of interest. It suggests that it is within this encounter that prejudices, unfairness and discriminatory values, attitudes and behaviours are played out. Chapter 7 examines the range of skills and knowledge utilised in anti-discriminatory practice and the application of these skills in practice. Chapter 8 attempts to integrate anti-discriminatory practice with a (limited) number of methods and approaches utilised in social work. The aim is to discuss and consider the applicability of anti-discriminatory practice ideas in some of the different methods and approaches generally used in social work. Chapter 9 discusses the dynamic nature of anti-discriminatory practice. It focuses on some of the service areas such as: children and families; adult services; disability; mental health and community development, and suggests that there are continuous changes taking place in social work practice and, therefore, anti-discriminatory practice would need to adapt and cope with the changing socio-cultural landscape. Finally, Chapter 10 discusses some complex sets of ideas about identity, meaning, culture and trust. It explores the inherent tensions in anti-discriminatory practice and argues that for the concept to remain relevant it has to continuously argue its case and reassert its effectiveness. This chapter suggests a new practice dimension and asserts the importance of an integrated approach that recognises the complexities of people's lives and the realities of their experiences.

Although there is a logical order to the book, each chapter is self-contained and could therefore be read out of sequence. It is evident that throughout the publication reference is made, in discussion, about how a particular area may be approached. However, it is important to stress that this is not a practice guideline with endless case examples; rather it is a starting point for rediscovering and reengaging with anti-discriminatory practice. We hope it is of use to you.

introduction

Part One
Underpinning Ideas
and Concepts

The Nature of Discrimination

Introduction
Key concepts
Overt discrimination
Covert discrimination
Individual level discrimination
Organisation discrimination
Colour blind approach
Reasoning
Conclusion

INTRODUCTION

It may be unsurprising, and indeed an obvious starting point, but it is important to begin a publication about key concepts in anti-discriminatory practice by acknowledging from the outset that discrimination does exist. Accepting the existence of discrimination in society is important because it sends a clear signal of openness and the ability to look beyond one's own experiences. The point is to assert and reinforce the fact that individual(s) and/or groups who claim that they are victims of discriminatory practices are not necessarily imagining things. Equally, it is important to recognise that simply because individual(s) and/or groups have not felt the full force of discrimination, or are not able to point to instances when they have been subjected to discrimination, it should not be assumed that they have somehow been spared the ignominy of discriminatory practices. As Pitts (2008) said (during a private conversation), 'because you are in a shelter does not mean you are not being bombed'. Of course, what makes the situation even more complicated is that there are people who, either genuinely or as a means of gaining the upper hand against their opponents, misinterpret all actions and reactions towards them as discriminatory. Leaving aside this latter group, the point being made is that it is important to acknowledge from the outset that discrimination is not an abstract concept that only exists in the minds of those who are experiencing it, but its impact is tangible and its affect on individual(s) and groups is profound. Just as importantly, discrimination has a major effect on social relationships between individuals and groups in society.

According to Payne, 'Discrimination means identifying individuals and groups with certain characteristics and treating them less well than people or groups with conventionally valued characteristics' (2005: 272). Thompson also picked up the attributive aspect of discrimination and defines it as:

> At its most basic level, discrimination is simply a matter of identifying differences and can be positive and negative. ... However, negative discrimination involves not only identifying differences but also making a negative attribution – attaching a negative or detrimental label or connotation to the person, group or entity concerned. That is, a question of certain individuals or groups being discriminated against. (2003a: 10)

Although both Payne and Thompson provide a very neat definition of what discrimination means, there is however little hint of the psychological, physical and emotional impact of discrimination on both those who are subjected to discrimination and those who are perpetrators. It is generally the case that when looking at discrimination the focus tends to be on who *said* what, when, in what manner and under what circumstance. Alternatively, there is great interest in knowing who exactly *did* what to whom, when and where. The incident itself and the language used before, during and after becomes the main line of enquiry rather than the impact of the incident on the individual(s) or groups concerned. Focusing attention on the incident itself and trying to discover the culprits does at least provide a tangible area of enquiry to address. But in our view it is just as important to take account of and consider the impact of discrimination on those affected by it.

As already implied, discrimination has a profound effect on one's physical, psychological and emotional state. It encourages mistrust, causes anxiety and unsettles one's sense of well-being. It can destroy confidence and affects one's sense of identity and relationship with others in society. Discrimination has the ability, for a period, to induce a sense of powerlessness that forces the individual or groups to re-evaluate their place in the world. At its worst, discrimination numbs the senses and can cause physical, psychological and emotional impotence. It exposes the fragility of the human spirit and highlights the important role that social interaction plays in shaping people's lives. What discrimination also lays bare is that other people's attitudes, views and behaviour do matter and that how people act towards each other creates feelings that make people question their sense of being in society. Giddens made the point that 'In daily social life, we normally give a good deal of attention to protecting or "saving" each other's "face"' (1989: 93). As made clear elsewhere (Okitikpi and Aymer 2008: 31), 'this is, to some extent, a reworking of Goffman's (1971) *civil inattention analysis*, which holds that people are connected to society by cordiality and a (unspoken) code of expectations. The cordiality and the code enable people to link to particular groups and at the same time live alongside others in society'. One of the outcomes of discrimination is that it breeds suspicion and distrust between individuals and groups. It strips individual(s) and groups of mutual respect and prevents them from developing a better understanding of each other. The breakdown of trust and connections between people is not conducive to the protective face-saving interactions that Giddens mentioned in his analysis. This social interaction device is not afforded to those that are discriminated against. Discrimination acts as a sieve and a way of differentiating and reinforcing the prevailing and dominant socio-cultural values. As Thompson (2006) acknowledged, there are of course two different kinds of discrimination, positive and negative. We are primarily concerned with negative discrimination because it is this that produces negative effects on people's lives.

One of the social effects of discrimination is that it excludes people from taking part in or enjoying that which is readily available to others in society. Because, as a matter of course, people are treated unfairly, they are not given or provided with the same opportunities as that enjoyed by everyone else. For example, the contention is that discrimination still exists and can be found within all aspects of the education system, the legal system, in housing, in business, in manufacturing, in the police and armed forces, in politics, in social welfare services provisions and in health care provisions (Kai 2003; Moonie et al. 2004). In essence, we would argue that despite the incredible social changes that have occurred in society, discrimination is still very much evident in all areas of society.

It is uncontroversial to assert that despite various legislation (see Chapter 5), and the social advancements that have been made in society towards equal opportunity, an individual's race/ethnicity, social class, gender, sexual orientation, impairment, age and religious affiliation still affects both their life chances and the level and kinds of opportunities available to them in society. In other words, despite advancement in the development of equal opportunity policies and the better protection afforded to people who are subjected to discriminatory and unfair practices, inequalities and discriminations have not been eradicated nor have they diminished. The fact is that, in general, working-class people, women, minority ethnic groups, particularly black people and people from South Asia (India, Pakistan, Bangladesh), lesbian and gay people, and people with impairments still face formidable obstacles in society. As a group, they continue to experience many disadvantages and discriminations in many areas of their lives. For example, at a basic level, women still experience the glass ceiling in employment, their salaries are less than their male colleagues in comparable occupations, they are more likely to undertake a greater share of child care responsibilities, and they continue to experience a higher level of domestic violence and sexual harassment. Black and South Asian people (particularly those from Pakistan and Bangladesh) have a higher level of unemployment in comparison to other groups, and black children, particularly African-Caribbean young men, are likely to leave school with little or no qualifications and are over-represented in the psychiatric and penal system. People with impairments often face segregation from an early age by either being placed in institutions or schooled separately from their peers. Working-class people, particular white boys, generally have poor educational prospects, are concentrated in high-density social environments, and are likely to be in low-skill employment.

KEY CONCEPTS

Although *discrimination* is used as an all-encompassing term to cover different kinds of discriminatory practices, it is important to de-construct (in the loose and lay sense of the word) the term in order to understand how they are manifested in day-to-day practices. The key concepts are overt and covert discrimination, individual discrimination and organisation discrimination.

OVERT DISCRIMINATION

Overt discrimination is easily identifiable because it is openly displayed and it operates at a basic and, some may say, crude level. The 'no blacks, no dogs and no Irish' signs displayed in windows by some landlords in parts of Britain during the 1950s are perhaps a good illustration of this. A further example is women being told their promotional prospects will be damaged because they are likely to take a career break to start a family. More generally, other examples includes wheelchair users being refused admission on to aeroplanes, or into cinemas and theatres because they are viewed as safety hazards; an older man whose wife had to go into hospital and who was offered the service of homehelp, meals-on-wheels and a volunteer visitor while a woman whose husband went into hospital was not offered the same services; and there are examples of local authorities not considering lesbian and gay couples/individuals as suitable foster parents because of their sexual orientation. Somerville and Steele (2002) highlighted the history of discrimination experienced by black people and other minority ethnic groups within the social housing market, particularly their clustering in dilapidated inner-city housing stocks. In relation to age, although there is legislation (The Employment Equality (Age) Regulations 2006) to prevent age discrim- ination, there is still a widespread assumption that age 65 years is the cut-off point by which people should be expected to stay in work. However, there are some exceptions to the idea of an age until which people should expect to work. For example, in the legal profession and board of directors of companies, 70 is regarded as the cut-off age and once an individual reaches such an age, they are expected to retire. In this respect, very little consideration is given to the capabilities and capacity of the individual concerned; rather it is their chronological age that is the over-riding determinant of how they are perceived. At the other end of the age range, young people wearing hoodies, including young white men, young black men and young southern Asian men (particularly Bangladeshi and Pakistani Muslims) face a greater level of scrutiny by the police and the security forces than others in society. There is an assumption, rightly or wrongly, that these groups are more likely to commit certain crimes (for example, car theft, street robberies, burglaries, violent offences and terrorist-related offences) compared to the rest of the population.

Of course, there are many examples of service users displaying *overt* discrimination towards practitioners. For example, service users refusing to have a black or Asian worker as their carer or key worker. There are other examples, including service users abusing, threatening or refusing to engage with workers because of their religion, accent, ethnicity, age and gender or because of their particular impairment. There is anecdotal evidence from black barristers and solicitors who relate that they are often confronted by white (and in some cases black) appellants who say openly and directly that they do not want to be represented by a black advocate.

COVERT DISCRIMINATION

Unlike overt discrimination, *covert* discrimination is a far more subtle kind of discrimination. It operates beneath the surface and involves deliberate acts of deception. Because of the form it takes, those who experience it find it far more difficult. However, despite its subtle nature, the emotional and psychological damage that is caused to the people concerned is not any different to the cruder overt version. Covert discrimination sometimes requires more guile and deception by the perpetrators. For example, workers who have not been employed in a post to which they are qualified are of course not told that they have been unsuccessful because of their age, sexual orientation, religious affiliation, nationality and gender. Instead they are given a more palatable and non-discriminating reason for not employing them. The open explanation is often that they were just unfortunate not to have got the post but that they were very close indeed. They are further told that they missed out to a very good candidate who was more successful at the interview. Covert discrimination is also manifested by not acknowledging any positive contributions people make or are making in the organisation in which they are employed. Brockes (2001) cites the experiences of Helena Dennison, chair of City Women's Network, who commented that people's (women) contributions in organisation are often undermined, and snide and derogative remarks are made about their appearances or their abilities. By its sheer nature, covert discrimination is a lot more difficult to prove by those experiencing it. It is generally the case that victims of covert discrimination find it difficult to provide the necessary concrete evidence that support the fact that they have been subjected to discriminatory practices. Many people who experience discriminatory practices often say they prefer to deal with overt discrimination because, in many ways, it is a lot more honest and transparent and the dividing lines are much clearer. In particular, they have a clearer sense about who to trust and who to be wary of within their organisation. Sometimes covert discrimination is so embedded within organisations and institutional structures, systems and processes that it has become institutionalised.

INDIVIDUAL LEVEL DISCRIMINATION

Clearly, as it is individuals who perpetrate discrimination and it is individuals who implement policies and carry out the aims and objectives of organisations, it is of no surprise that it is at the individual level that the nature of discrimination is brought into sharp focus. Individual-level discrimination can be both verbal and non-verbal and it can be intentional or unintentional – the important point is how it is experienced by the people at the receiving end. Non-verbal communications take on an added significance when looking at individual-level discrimination. In this domain, body posture, eye contact, aura (vibes) and gestures all convey meanings and, rightly or wrongly, they are elevated to mean far more than ordinarily would be the case. Those who experience this form of discrimination report that they become extremely skilled in its detection. Similarly, language and language use come under closer scrutiny. It is through actions and language that discriminations are perpetuated and reinforced. As a result, what is said, how it is said and the general impressions that are conveyed are all very important. It is always difficult to be prescriptive about which words to use at any one time, because part of the difficulty is that words change, as do their meaning. A word that may be deemed acceptable today may quickly fall out of fashion for whatever reason. But language and words do matter and they have a negative impact on those who feel discriminated against. As Roberts, Davies and Jupp asserted:

> Language not only reflects and transmits the values and relationships of a society; it actively creates and maintains them. So all the time we are getting things done with language; we are creating a piece of social reality (Berger and Luckman 1967), in the sense that we are making relationships and establishing roles and identities in the choices of language we make and our orientation to the world consists, in part, in our language behaviour. We are also acting out the social systems and structures which helps us, as a society, to order the world and make sense of it even if, as with many power structures we do not benefit from it. (Roberts, Davies and Jupp (1992) quoted in Thompson 2003b: 73)

Thompson (2003b) recognised the significance of language and the power dynamics inherent in the interaction between people. In highlighting the power of language, Thompson further observed that:

> 'one problem with developing a sensitivity to the discrimination potential of language is that this complex area is often over-simplified and

trivialised. Many people see it as a simple matter of identifying certain 'bad' words (such as 'chairman' or 'blackleg') and trying to avoid them, without necessarily understanding why they should be avoided. (Thompson 2003b: 71)

Thompson's observation is significant because it acknowledges the importance of language and at the same time it encourages an examination of why words matter. Implicit in his assertion is the view that, rather than feeling defensive because certain words are now deemed offensive (for example, is it acceptable to call women *love, pet, darling*? Is it ok to say black coffee or blackboard? *Chairman? Manhole cover?* Should it be history or herstory? And should Human and Woman be changed?), a productive way forward would be to try and explore why the terms or words are no longer deemed to be acceptable. The plea from Thompson, it seems to us, is for tolerance and a certain degree of empathy towards those who are or may be offended by the words or terms that are used. Another reason why the individual-level discrimination is worth considering is because how an individual feels at the end of an encounter would be largely due to how they have been (mis)treated by the other person. If an individual holds negative views about others, for example that black people are less intelligent than white people, men are superior to women or that lesbian and gay people are cursed and face damnation for their 'unnatural' sexual practices, then these discriminatory attitudes are bound to affect, negatively, any relationship that is developed with people from those groups. It is unrealistic and somewhat disingenuous to believe that one's view, attitudes and beliefs have no influences on one's action. Many practitioners and students profess that although they may hold certain negative views about individuals or groups, they would not allow these views to affect their practice. It is worth noting that individuals can 'leak' their true feelings, particularly to those who are sensitised to detect them.

However, having asserted that individuals perpetuate discriminatory practices, it is worth acknowledging Vivian and Brown's point that:

The problem, very simply, is that analysis of individual personalities cannot account for the large-scale social behaviour that normally characterises prejudices and intergroup conflict more generally. If it were true that prejudices derived from disorder in personality, then we would expect the expression of prejudices or discrimination within groups to vary as much as the personality of members comprising the group. But in fact the evidence seems to indicate that prejudices within groups is often remarkably uniform. (1995: 59)

Despite Vivian and Brown's caution, what is being suggested here is that in highlighting individual-level discrimination, we recognise that discrimination does not just appear out of the ether. Rather it is made to happen by individuals or groups of people acting in a way that is detrimental to others. Also within Vivian and Brown's assertion is a tendency to absolve individuals of their responsibilities and as a result the problem of discrimination appears to be externalised.

ORGANISATION DISCRIMINATION

Although it is our contention that it is individuals, either acting alone or in groups, who act in a way that is discriminatory, their actions and attitudes may be encouraged or endorsed by institutions and organisations. The Macpherson report into the death of Stephen Lawrence is helpful in this regard. He suggested that institutional racism is a:

> collective failure of an organisation to provide an appropriate and professional service to people because of their colour, culture or ethnic origin. It can be seen or detected in processes, attitudes and behaviour which amount to discrimination through unwitting prejudice, ignorance, thoughtlessness and racist stereotyping which disadvantage minority ethnic people. (Macpherson 1999: 6.4)

While the Macpherson report focused, to a large extent, on how race influenced police (in)actions and reactions in the killing of Stephen Lawrence by racist white youths, it is also possible to extrapolate from his definition of how institutions and organisations could, by omission and commission, discriminate through their systems, cultures and processes. Clearly organisations and institutions are more than the sum total of the people who occupy the various positions within them. It is well recognised that all organisations and institutions after a period develop ethos, values and cultures that transcend the people that work in them. Handy (2005) explored the ways that organisations develop cultural patterns that enable its members to work as a group and gel together. Institutions and organisations develop a pattern and ways of doing things that enable them to function. All members are then expected to accept and adhere to the assumptions and behaviours that have now become the established ways of doing things. Although these discriminatory attitudes and behaviours are not written down in any organisational or institutional manual, nevertheless, all members are expected to abide by its unspoken culture. The power of such cultures is difficult to quantify or convey, however members who go against it may find themselves ostracised and made to feel uncomfortable at best and outsiders at worst. The effect of culture upon an organisation or institution should not be underestimated. Cultures should not necessarily be viewed negatively because they act as the glue for binding organisations, institutions and its people together. At its best, organisational and institutional culture creates an important bond among staff and helps the development of an ethos and ways of doing things that enable aims and objects to be met. But they are also the means by which discriminations and discriminatory practices are continued. The issue is also about changing the culture from one that is discriminatory to one which fosters anti-discriminatory practices.

COLOUR BLIND APPROACH

Many may regard it as unfair and perhaps irrational to place people who are unaware and treat people the same (colour blind approach) under the same heading as *overt, covert, individual discrimination and organisation discrimination*. The argument would be that unlike the above-mentioned, the colour blind appproach has a different rationale and motivation. Taking such an approach is based on an attempt to be fair and just. Those who profess this approach do not believe in discriminating against people but start from the premise that people should be treated the same irrespective of their background, age, gender and whether they have impairment or not. The basic principle being that by ignoring differences and not taking account of any of the areas that are the causes of discriminatory practices then people are being judged on merits and their personality and nothing else. However, the reason for including the colour blind approach is that, as has already been demonstrated, discrimination occurs not just by active intention to discriminate but by omission and lack of consideration given to the consequences of actions and reactions. In other words, not taking account of difference far from guaranteeing a fair and just approach could actually be reinforcing the discriminatory practices that are already in existence.

This approach presupposes that all encounters between people are devoid of any historical baggage and that it is possible to relate to people on a one-to-one level without the background 'noises', that are ever present, getting in the way. In this instance, the background noises relate to the historical legacies that contribute to the way people relate to and

key concepts in anti-discriminatory social work

interact with each other. So, for example, when white and black people meet, overhanging the relationship is the historical and contemporary realities of colonialism and racism; when men and women meet, sexual politics and gender relations lace the interaction and is evident from the outset in the way language is used (Spender 1990; Tannen 1995). There is an assumption that people with impairment are not capable of operating at the same intellectual and social level as others in society. In this respect, the situation is not helped by the fact that the physical environment is essentially designed for those without impairment. Similarly, despite evidence to the contrary, a widespread view still prevails that equates old age with being, inevitably, a time of decline, as a period when people are a burden on the state and a time when people's intellectual faculties are impaired and people are incapable of making decisions for themselves (Crawford and Walker 2004).

In essence, the attempt to ignore these background noises, while well meaning, is unrealistic because people are not only shaped by their identity and individual biographies but have pre-existing narratives that contribute to the ways people see themselves and to the ways in which they relate to other people and to the world around them. Epston and White's (1990) work is helpful in this respect because it encapsulates the idea that people do not exist in a vacuum but that the views and attitudes that others have about them, overt or covert, impact on their self-identity and their sense of place in the world. So what is being suggested is that the colour blind approach not only ignores the inherent differences that already exist between people but, as a consequence, it could be argued that it fails to understand the ways these differences shape lives and all social interactions and relationships.

Another variation in the theme of the colour blind approach is where those who are discriminated against refuse, either intentionally or unintentionally, to acknowledge that the reactions towards them are as a result of their age, colour, gender, sexual orientation or their impairment. Those who do not acknowledge the impact of discrimination in their life, for whatever reasons, are often thought to be living under false consciousness or they have internalised the negative experiences to such a degree that they are no longer aware of them. Without getting distracted into the fog land of what may be described as psuedo-psychotherapeutic discourse and Marxist notion of 'false consciousness', the point is that what they both, in their different ways, alert us to is the ways in which ideology and/or personal biography may distort our perceptions of 'reality' and how an inaccurate perception of self has developed through the internalisation of (*negative*) social structures (Waddington 1974).

REASONING

The reasons for discrimination are multiple and they could range from people who have philosophical and/or political perspectives to those who passionately believe that there are fundamental biological, cultural and intellectual differences between people. Accordingly, there is a sense that rather than chiding those who discriminate against others, there should be a recognition, as with 'positive discrimination', that people are merely exercising a choice, a preference for one particular group over others and these preferences are based on likes and dislikes and on similarities and shared norms and values (Pinker 2002). Other reasons could include cultural connection and a sense of affiliation because of ethnicity, gender, sexual orientation and impairment. In addition, people are driven to act in particular ways for different reasons and while it is always dangerous to ascribe motives to people, there are often explanations, however distasteful, for their discriminatory attitude. For example, there are black defendants (and white defendants) who do not want to be represented by a black advocate. Their explanation is that they believe they stand a far better chance of acquittal if they were represented by a white advocate. One explanation could be that far from believing that black barristers and solicitors are less able than their white counterpart, the rationale is that because the courts and criminal justice system is perceived as discriminatory in its practices, particularly against certain sections of people in society, then the defendants may believe that it is better to have a representative who is likely to be 'more' acceptable to the 'system', hence their preference for a white advocate.

One of the complications when looking at the whole area of discrimination is that there are many people who genuinely believe that they do not discriminate in their personal life or in their professional dealings with colleagues and service users yet they have been subjected to vilification and abuse for asserting their belief. They have been the subjects of 'hate campaigns' either because of their use of words that are deemed unacceptable or they have voiced their views openly that they do not believe in treating people differently or taking account of differences. Listening to the laments of those who have experienced abuse and criticism from their co-workers because of their perceived lack of understanding and awareness of the intricacies of discrimination, one is struck by the incongruity of both sides. But there is an irony in that those who believe in equality, fairness and a just society should display such arrogance and intolerant behaviour and attitudes towards others who may not be so well schooled in the area of anti-discriminatory practice.

As was mentioned earlier, all these forms of discriminatory practices operate differently but we would argue that the impact on those who are at the receiving end is perhaps not so different. The important point is that there is a need to deconstruct the nature of discrimination, consider how it operates, how it is perpetuated and to understand its impact on those who experience it.

CONCLUSION

In conclusion, discrimination, if it is allowed to exist unchallenged, saps people of their confidence, dignity and self-respect. It is a demeaning experience that forces people to look at themselves and consider their sense of place in the world. The powerlessness that discrimination inflicts on its victims is tangible and could, literally, destroy an individual and/or a collective's will. In discussing the nature of discrimination, the aim is to provide an important backdrop for exploring the key concepts in anti-discriminatory practice. As we have tried to demonstrate, discrimination affects people in most damaging ways and it perpetuates a hierarchical structure based on nothing but an outdated socio-biological determinism tinged with a socially constructed binary worldview. In looking at the nature of discrimination, in the first instance, the attempt was to connect the concept to experiences and then explore the models of practice that have developed, the theoretical frameworks that inform anti-discriminatory practice and a shift in paradigm towards a new practice dimension.

Points to ponder

Exercise 1

- As well as the equal opportunity policies, what else could organisations do to create conducive environments for anti-discriminatory practice to thrive in?

(Continued)

(Continued)

- Is it worthwhile and productive to take account of the psychological and emotional effects of discrimination or should the focus be on the incidents that occurred and the attitudes and behaviours that were displayed?
- While overt discrimination is easily identifiable, covert discrimination presents a far more difficult concept to unravel. Is covert discrimination all about interpretation and people being unnecessarily over-sensitive and could this area of discrimination ever be resolved?

Exercise 2

- Is discrimination only in the minds of the victims?
- What are the effects of discrimination on the people who experience it?
- Is it only men who can be sexist?
- Could black and Asian people be racists too or is it only white people?
- Is treating everyone the same the best way to tackle discrimination?

2
Ideas Informing Anti-discriminatory Practice Models

Introduction
Ideas informing anti-discriminatory practice
Key concepts
Socio-structural understanding
Anti-discriminatory dilemma
The hierarchy of oppression
Conclusion

INTRODUCTION

The social work profession has fought hard to highlight and challenge discriminations, injustices and inequalities that pervade much of its practices. Since it embarked on this path in the 1970s, we would argue much has changed. The profession now demands an approach (a way of working) that is both inclusive and non-discriminatory. In its definition of social work, the British Association of Social Workers (BASW) said:

> The social work profession promotes social change, problem solving in human relationships and the empowerment and liberation of people to enhance wellbeing. Utilising theories of human behaviour and social systems, social work intervenes at the points where people interact with their environments. Principles of human rights and social justice are fundamental to social work. (BASW – Code of Ethics 2001: 1)

Underscoring this definition is the recognition that change is possible and that, despite life's vicissitudes, people are neither static beings nor mere puppets of their social environment. Rather, there is an underlying belief that it is possible for people to reactivate their coping capabilities and regain control of all aspects of their life having been given the necessary help and support. The presumption is that because people experience difficulties or may have suffered misfortunes, it does not mean that they should lose the right to make choices about areas that affect their lives. What BASW's definition also implies is that social work intervenes at the point where people are either having difficulties in their lives and are therefore not able to function effectively without social welfare intervention or that they may need emotional, practical help and/or support. So from the very beginning of their involvement with social services, there is recognition, by practitioners, that service users are at a disadvantage. For the practitioner, the service user's vulnerability is just one area of consideration, albeit an important one. In addition, the other areas of consideration are of course the vulnerability the service user may face because of who they are. In other words, their age, class, sexual orientation, religious affiliation, race, impairment and gender would also need to be taken into account.

In recognition of service users' vulnerability and the fact that they are at a disadvantage in their relationship with professionals, anti-discriminatory practice demands that practitioners should not practice in a way that either reinforces the discrimination or oppression that people already experience or create an environment that enables such practices to continue. It is therefore a way of working that encourages both introspection and a pro-active approach on the part of the practitioner.

Lavalette and Penketh chided the fact that social work, as a profession, has lost its direction because the work is now: 'shaped by managerialism, by the fragmentation of services, by financial restrictions and lack of resources, by increased bureaucracy and workloads, by the domination of care management performance indicators, and the increased use of private sector' (2006: 3). The concerns being expressed by these authors are about the negative direction of social work practice and the over dominance of a bureaucratic market-based approach. Implicit in their criticism is the fear that social work has become an instrument for perpetuating inequalities and that the general approach adopted by practitioners has become mechanical and distant.

At some level, while there is general understanding of what it means to do 'good' and try and attempt to make a difference in people's lives, it is our contention that there are often confusions, at a basic level, of what anti-discriminatory practice actually involves and what is expected of those who want to integrate it into their practice (Okitikpi and Aymer 2008). In our view, while different models of anti-discriminatory practice exist, it is not apparent that they are necessarily clear or generally understood by those who try to put them into practice. Often, the situation is not helped by the fact that there is not one body of knowledge that can be referred to that can provide an all-encompassing explanation or framework of the approach. Rather, there is a range of theories, ideas and concepts that are both complementary and sometimes competing and contradictory. In other words, the underpinning theoretical ideas that inform anti-discriminatory practice straddle different perspectives and hang between competing theoretical ideas. While it is not necessary to have knowledge of sociology, politics, psychology or philosophy in order to practice in a way that is anti-discriminatory, it would enhance understanding and enable practitioners to appreciate the principles and theories that inform both anti-discriminatory practice and some of the other ideas that are explored in this chapter.

IDEAS INFORMING ANTI-DISCRIMINATORY PRACTICE

As already mentioned, there is no all-encompassing theory from which ADP developed; rather, as Okitikpi and Aymer observed:

> it gets its coherence and framework by borrowing from a range of disciplines. In other words anti-discriminatory practice theory is an amalgam, or hybrid of different ideas. The disciplines, ideas and concepts that inform ADP include sociology, anthropology, social economics, social psychology and political theory. (2008: 34)

Again, they highlighted the fact that:

> The philosophical underpinning of anti-discriminatory practice can of course be traced back to Western European's 17th century enlightenment movement. The realisation that human beings are not mere conduits of pre-ordained ways of being and that human beings can determine their future opened up great possibilities. The shift from the paradigm which assumed that people were encased in a pre-destined world to one which hailed free will and the ability of human being to shape their existence (as well as their future) was momentous. Rather than the presumed rights of certain people to rule over others there was talk of: 'Man was born free …', and 'Those who think themselves the masters of others are indeed greater slaves than they. (Rousseau, cited in Cranston 1968: 59 in Okitikpi and Aymer 2008: 32)

Anti-discriminatory practice is about developing a way of working that is not based on bias, prejudices, discrimination, injustice or unfair treatment. It is an approach which calls for people to be treated with respect and holds that people should *not* be treated badly or unfairly because of their race, gender, sexual orientation, impairment, class (be it middle class or working class), religious belief or age. Apart from how people should be treated, ADP requires a certain degree of introspection in order to be appreciative of the kinds of negative attitudes and beliefs that foster prejudicial views and discriminatory actions that are ultimately manifested in day-to-day practices. Unsurprisingly, there is an assumption that it is difficult to separate actions and behaviours from previous experiences, thoughts, feelings and attitudes. The influence of thoughts in action is of course well recognised in the profession. Indeed, methods of intervention such as crisis intervention, task-centered, cognitive-behavioural and psychoanalytical approaches all recognise the importance and impact of experience, thoughts, feelings and attitudes on people's behaviour. These influences are relevant and they are as applicable to service users as they are to practitioners.

The attempt to tackle discriminatory practices has taken many different forms over the years. At some point, the focus was on changing people's perceptions and/or attitudes towards others. There were attempts at changing people's discriminatory behaviours and the negative assumptions that may underlie their behaviour. Finally, towards the later part of the 20th century, the emphasis shifted away from changing people's values, perceptions and attitudes towards enacting legislations that would entrench anti-discriminatory principles and ideals in practices. Although the emphasis has shifted towards a legislative and Human Rights based approach, we believe practitioners are still primarily driven by a fundamental belief in 'doing good' and doing what they consider to be the right thing in order to improve people's life chances. For them, it is about economic, social and political justice as well as fairness and equality for all. For many practitioners, developing and maintaining an ethical and anti-discriminatory practice approach is their driving force rather than merely adhering to the legal requirement.

KEY CONCEPTS

Anti-discriminatory practice is based on the notion of social justice and that it is possible to treat people fairly and not view or react negatively towards them as a result of some preconceived ideas. Although the idea that underlies anti-discriminatory practice is relatively simple and, some may say, self-evident and logical, the concept continues to walk a tightrope between competing discourses. For example, anti-discriminatory practice really, in our view, took root in the 1960s following the struggle for black liberation (both in the United States and in Britain) and the call from the women's movement for a better recognition of women's rights. Although the ADP concept began in the 1960s (as mentioned in the Introduction, Forsythe (1995) dates it further back), we would argue it was fully developed in the 1980s and 1990s, as previously mentioned, and that its philosophical base could be traced back to the European Enlightenment period. However, it is evident that the concept has taken different forms and it has had to withstand competing political ideologies (i.e., socialism, liberalism, conservatism, capitalism and multiculturalism) as well as socio-cultural discourses (such as *modernity, functionalism, structuralism, post-structuralism and post-modernity*). Born in the modernist meta-narrative era when concepts and ideas were deemed to have universal application and when there was such a thing as universal truth, anti-discriminatory practice has continued to try to remain relevant in a changing social, economic, cultural and political landscape. Once introduced into the practice arena, anti-discriminatory practice flourished (to a greater or lesser degree) in different political environments. It was not always the case that left-leaning organisations were the only environments in which anti-discriminatory practices were given opportunity to take root (although the concept was more readily accepted in left-leaning organisations). By its sheer nature (promoting fairness, justice, treating people without prejudice, non-discriminatory attitude) and the pioneering zeal of many of its proponents, anti-discriminatory practices developed in some of the most unlikely places. For example, anti-discriminatory practices were to be found as much in socialist and liberal-leaning organisations as in conservative-orientated organisations and in some business-sector organisations as well. It is as prominent and effective in social democratic societies as it is in social welfare capitalist societies. In other words, it would be a misconception to believe that only in left-leaning multicultural societies or organisations (or local authorities) can anti-discriminatory practice be developed and practised.

SOCIO-STRUCTURAL UNDERSTANDING

Modernity is essentially the culmination of a period that is termed the early modern era and is dated to have begun in the late 15th century and ending, according to some commentators, in the 20th century. The period covered three of the most momentous events in the history of humankind. The early modern period saw the beginning of colonialism, the Enlightenment and the start of the industrial revolution. By the close of the 20th century, the advancements (particularly in the Western world) in medicine, education, science, economic and social developments were profound. These momentous events not only changed the world, they irrevocable changed the very nature of the relationship between people and their world. Modernity has been described as, essentially, a cultural and intellectual movement. The term denotes a particular worldview in which there was a belief in the capacity of human beings not only to influence and shape their world but also to change it. Guided by teleological ideals (a philosophical school of thought that believes that there is a final goal or purpose for all things that exist), the movement attempted to provide an all-encompassing explanation of all aspects of human existence. Modernity holds that not only are there discernable truths but that these truths are universal and therefore applicable to all. Within modernity, there were of course many other movements and ideas that challenged the presumptions upon which modernity is built. For example, functionalism, structuralism, post-tructuralism and post-modernity all laid claim to a much better explanation or analysis of the cultural, social, intellectual and physical environment.

At a basic level, *functionalism* posits that it is important to recognise that things exist in society for a purpose. In essence, something exists because it serves an important function and is therefore necessary to the society. In other words, it could be argued that discrimination, oppression and inequalities exist in society because they serve a purpose. Although functionalism originated from the work of the sociology pioneer Auguste Comte, it was later developed, to a limited degree, by Emile Durkeim and, more extensively, by Talcott Parsons and Robert Merton. It was anthropologists such as Alfred Radcliffe-Brown, Bronislaw Malinowski and Margaret Mead who really turned functionalism from a speculative doctrine into an applied discipline. Functionalism stresses the interdependence of society and asserts that the coherence and cohesion of any society depends on the effective working of its component parts. As Giddens observed:

> To study the function of a social practice or institution is to analyse the contribution which that practice or institution makes to the continuation of the society as a whole. The best way to understand this is by analogy

to the human body, a comparison which Comte, Durkeim and many subsequent functionalist authors make. To study a bodily organ, like the heart, we need to show how it relates to other parts of the body. Pumping blood around the body, the heart plays a vital role in the continuation of the life of the organism. Similarly, analysing the function of a social item means showing the part it plays in the continued existence of a society. (Giddens 1989: 696)

Rightly, in our opinion, there is a tacit acknowledgement that there is such a thing as society and all its components parts, however insignificant they may seem, contribute to its continuing existence. Although functionalism is essentially concerned with the effects of social behaviour, it is not particularly interested in the causes or motives of that behaviour. This has an echo of the approach that currently dominates the idea that has been adopted to tackle discriminatory practices. For example, at some point, it was deemed important to look at people's behaviour and to challenge the attitudes and thoughts that encourage discriminatory and oppressive practices. So if one was to follow the logic of functionalism, then it could be argued that anti-discriminatory practice exists in order to enable society to function effectively and for all its component parts to act in the best interest of society.

While functionalism is interested, to some extent, in maintaining and preserving the social order, *structuralism* attempts to provide a deeper level of explanation about the inner workings of structures. Structuralism, like many of the other social discourses, is a complex concept that does not necessarily lend itself to easy explanation. Based on the work of Ferdinand de Saussure (1857–1913), and further developed by Michel Foucault (who straddles both structuralism and post-structuralism) and Jacques Lacan, its starting point is that in order to analyse any particular field of human science, it is important to understand that all structures are complex systems of interrelated parts. Assiter (1984) suggested it is possible to discern at least four tenets of structuralism. For example, structuralists:

- believe the whole (structure) is determined by the elements within it;
- believe that every system has a structure;
- are not particularly interested in changes that happen in systems; instead they focus on 'structural' laws that deal with coexistence in systems;
- believe the 'real things' lie beneath the surface or the appearance of meaning.

This latter point that the 'real things' lie beneath the surface or the appearance of meaning is important in anti-discriminatory practice because much of the discussion about discrimination is that it is both explicit and implicit, overt and covert (see Chapter 1). As discrimination operates at different levels, structuralism could help in providing a way of understanding the inner and hidden meanings about discrimination embedded in modern day language. Structuralism provides a way of 'reading' and understanding how culture generates and regenerates itself through the development of myths, shared meanings, symbols, signs and practices. Making a parallel point, Pierre Bourdieu highlighted the way class dominance is perpetuated and how this in turn shapes social relationships. In his view, the dominant class does not overtly dominate or conspire against other class groups in society but rather, as Lechte (1994: 45) observed, they are the 'beneficiary of economic, social and symbolic power'. In essence, the power that enables the dominant class to maintain their position in society is embodied in what Bourdieu called 'economic and cultural capital, which in turn are not only embedded in society's institutions and practices but they are reproduced by these very institutions and practices' (Lechte 1994: 45). Bourdieu's analysis of power and dominance and his assertion about the role of economic and cultural capital in the perpetuation of class dominance is of great interest to us. Institutional racism, the glass ceiling, the medical model towards disability, coupled with the underachievement of black boys, the general poor outcomes for working-class white boys and the high level of social exclusion in society (these difficulties and obstacles) all reinforce the contention that discrimination is not just about individual prejudices but that there are institutional and structural dimensions to it as well.

In reaction against structuralism's explanations of social structures and the belief that individuals are shaped by the structures (sociology, psychology and language) in which they exist, *post-structuralists* take a more 'critical' approach. They move from mere explanation towards a more proactive critique and critical analysis of social sciences, including society and culture. The aim was not just to explain but to work towards the changing of society. As Foucault observed:

> For the last ten or fifteen years, [there has been] the immense and proliferating criticizability of things, institutions, practices, and discourses; a sort of general feeling that the ground was crumbling beneath our feet, especially in places where it seemed most familiar, most solid, and closest to us, to our

bodies, to our everyday gestures. But alongside this crumbling and the astonishing efficacy of discontinuous, particular, and local critiques, the facts were also revealing something ... beneath this whole thematic, through it and even within it, we have seen what might be called the insurrection of subjugated knowledges. (1976: 6)

Characterised by the works of the Frankfurt School, Foucault, Derrida and feminist critique, the focus was on the radical change of society and an integrated approach towards the sciences. The post-structuralists accepted structuralism's explanation of structures but they injected a critical and radical edge into their analysis. As they were under the umbrella of postmodernity, they rejected ideas that purported to provide an all-encompassing and universal truth and indeed questioned, in the case of Jacques Derrida, the very existence of truth itself. At its heart was the challenging of the premise (philosophical, epistemological and methodological) upon which modernity was built and the 'decentring' of knowledge and 'self'. Key to post-structuralist thinking is the idea that society and people are not on some progressive (teleology) trajectory that proceeds upwards towards some kind of zenith. Rather, the whole structure, system and 'self' are plagued by discontinuity, conflicting considerations, fragmentation, competing tensions and uncertainty. This idea, to some extent, dovetailed with social tensions that were clearly visible (culminating in the winter of discontent, race riots in some inner-city areas, concerns about the family and immigration, high levels of unemployment) in society during the 1970s and 1980s.

Post-modernity has a great deal in common with post-structuralism in challenging the presumptions and assumptions of a unified, progressive and co-existing social and world view. In their view, the explanations and answers provided through meta-narratives were no longer sustainable. For them, what constitutes knowledge and what could be defined as truth are not universal concepts that can be assumed and therefore considered to be applicable to all (Katz 1996; Clarke 1999; Thompson 2005). Discontinuity, fluidity, fragmentation, uncertainty and relativism could be described as the hallmark of post-modernity. Of course, there were sub-groups within the post-modernist's umbrella who explored different aspects of the concept. However, what united them all, to some extent, was the questioning of a unified entity and the critique of the idea of absolute truth and total knowledge. For example, in post-modernity, the subject became, literally, both central and peripheral to the discourse. Similarly, hybridity, acculturation, contradictions, irony and the localisation of history reinforced post-modernity's claim to distinctiveness from modernity. Post-modernity was not just a mere reaction against modernity, there was belief that the fundamental principles that characterised modernity could no longer be applied or sustained in a changing world where different voices and ideas were emerging. Post-modern ideas provided an opportunity for different voices to surface and to lay claim to different (but equally as important and relevant) knowledge and truth.

ANTI-DISCRIMINATORY DILEMMA

These competing voices and the differing ideas were and still are the background noise with which ADP has to compete. Anti-discriminatory practice has, in our view, had to struggle to keep its aims and objects in the face of all these competing demands and discourses. While it was the case that in the early period many commentators and practitioners focused much more on race and gender, it has had to be more encompassing by ensuring that all other areas of discrimination were tackled. The difficulty has been that discourses about modernity, post-structuralism and post-modernity/post-modernism gave a green light for a more relativistic approach towards anti-discriminatory practice. Rather than accepting the idea of universality in the area of anti-discriminatory practice, there was a tendency to challenge, not necessarily the existence of discrimination but, the extent to which one could assert that all forms of discrimination are wrong and unacceptable. For example, it is not uncommon for some who call for religious tolerance to be discriminatory against women, or for men who believe in sexual equality to treat their partners badly or for someone with impairment to be racist. In fact, many Muslim Imams and orthodox Jewish men do not touch women because women are deemed to be unclean. In Christianity, there are those who believe and proudly proclaim that the bible endorses the castigation of gays and lesbians.

Paradoxically, while post-modernity provided a philosophical underpinning for people to challenge the orthodoxy (about race, culture, age, impairment, religiosity, gender, sexuality and identity), it also gave people the confidence to question the relevance and importance of other forms of discrimination. In other words, the rejection of universality and grand narratives (providing the appropriate explanation and answers for all) enabled some within the anti-discriminatory practice movement to call into question the connection between themselves and others who also experienced discrimination. During the 1970s, 1980s and 1990s, the general approach towards anti-discriminatory practice was to focus on individuals' racial, sexual or gender identity and their affiliated groups. This was the period when the notion of society was questioned by the New Right, and there was valorisation of individualism and the encouragement of the politics of identity. During this era, when relativism reigned, the personal and political, the cultural and all besides were all subsumed under the control of the individual through the politics of identity.

Anti-discriminatory practice did not and does exist in a vacuum because, as well as its fundamental principles that guided it (as highlighted above), it was also reinforced by the development of multiculturalism. As Heywood observed:

> Multiculturalism is more an arena for ideological debate than an ideology in its own right. As an arena for debate, it encompasses a range of views about the implications of growing cultural diversity and, in particular, about how cultural differences can be reconciled with civic unity. Its key theme is therefore diversity within unity. (2007: 310)

The real difficulty for anti-discriminatory practice was how to stay true to its core value (of equality, open access, fairness, social and political justice, opportunity for all) while at the same time recognising difference and respecting diversity. Multiculturalism was interpreted to mean accepting difference and respecting diversity without questioning. The predominant view was that no one had the right to question how other cultural groups behave or comment on their mores and values. In other words, it was deemed imperative (it was indeed celebrated) that groups should be allowed to maintain their distinct cultural values and not necessarily attempt to integrate with the mainstream. The view was that as long as people within the groups obeyed the law, then they were free to either engage on their terms or disengage from the mainstream. The tension for ADP was therefore how to reconcile cultural practices that could be both damaging to people in their respective groups and perhaps counter-progressive in outlook – for example, regressive ideas about sexual orientation; women's role in the family and in society; views about childhood and childrearing practices; strong belief in predetermination of all human beings and therefore rejection of agency; negative attitudes towards disability; forced marriages; and an honour bound approach to dealing with disputes between and within families and groups. In some cases, the practices set back the progress and gains that had been achieved and they reinforced various forms of discrimination and oppressions. In our view, multiculturalism was misinterpreted to mean unconditional acceptance and positive regard of others' cultures and practices despite the fact that they may be incompatible with the values of an advanced liberal democracy. Furthermore, while some cultural practices may not necessarily violate the law, they may nevertheless be considered to be against the spirit, ethos and principle of ADP.

The reason that there should have been acquiescence with such counter-progressive attitudes and behaviours is difficult to understand, but Cohen (2008: 26) believes it may have something to do with European's (particularly the liberal middle class) 'cult of the authentic'. In our view, Cohen may have stumbled on an interesting observation that is worthy of further analysis. If indeed the cult of the authentic is the driving force, then it could provide an explanation as to why there is such emphasis on encouraging groups to remain within their cultural boundaries. This thinking actually discourages social integration because it valorises difference and diversity rather than celebrating similarities and championing social and cultural integration and the development of civil society. In our view, the cult of the authentic 'ghettoises' individuals and groups and views people in a lineal, uni-dimensional way and it does not appreciate the complex nature of identity, culture and social relationships.

THE HIERARCHY OF OPPRESSION

The outcome of this tendency towards individualism, politics of identity and the questioning of the existing approach was the development of what could only be described as a hierarchy of oppression. The hierarchy of oppression involves some people believing that their groups' discriminatory experiences are unique because it is more systematic, pernicious and institutionalised in comparison to others. In their view, because they suffer such a level of discrimination, they deserve a greater level of recognition and better understanding of their position in society. Moreover, they further suggested that as their discrimination was more visible (be it their colour, their gender and/or their impairment), they are unable to hide and are therefore far more vulnerable. This assertion suggests that people who experience discrimination because of their sexual orientation, religious belief, ethnicity (including travellers, Roma and Irish) and social class could buffer themselves against negative attitudes by remaining quiet about their background. This suggestion was not only ungracious, it further compounds the negative experiences of groups/individuals that were asked to keep 'silent'. In addition, it goes against the humanistic tendency that underlies ADP. Remaining silent about one's background in order not to attract discriminatory attitudes and negative treatment does not accord with ADP's staunch belief in equality for all, fairness, social and economic justice in society.

During the period in the 1980s and 1990s when individualism and the politics of identity were the driving forces in anti-discriminatory practice, many found it difficult to challenge reactionary and discriminatory attitudes by some people who had experienced discriminations. The concerns were that by challenging such behaviour and attitudes there was the danger of reinforcing, compounding and contributing to people's negative experiences. It would seem ironic that those who have experience of discrimination should suggest that others stay quiet about their experiences. For a period at least, many people did stay quiet as they were too afraid to let others know their pain and suffering in case they were accused of trying to highjack the concept.

CONCLUSION

This chapter has explored, albeit briefly, some concepts, socio-cultural ideas and a number of underpinning theoretical ideas that have informed anti-discriminatory practice. It discussed the fact that ADP straddles different perspectives and has to contend with competing ideas. The aim has been to highlight some of the complex dynamics that anti-discriminatory practice has to work within. We have tried to make the point that, although ADP is an empowering doctrine, there is a growing danger of it becoming hijacked by those who are intolerant, oppressive and discriminatory in their attitudes and beliefs. For example, there are those who fervently believe it is discriminatory to impose Western values (by this, they mean individualism, separation of state and religion, tolerance, equality, fairness, justice for all, equal opportunity, acceptance of homosexuality, child centeredness) on them. As well as demanding that their race, ethnicity, culture, identity, religious beliefs, class, gender and disability be taken into account, they believe it should be their right (should their culture or religious doctrine require it) to, effectively, discriminate against women, people with impairments, gay men and lesbians and ignore children's rights. It is our contention that ADP should be reclaimed and not be allowed to encourage separatism and/or intolerance.

In our view, two of the key aspects of anti-discriminatory practice are that the concept takes for granted the idea of universal application and the importance of recognising the level of inter-dependence that exists in society. It is not a pick-and-mix concept that exonerates those who experience discrimination from practising in a non-discriminatory way. It would be impossible, despite views to the contrary, to hold negative and discriminatory views about people and still work with them effectively. A religious fundamentalist who holds very negative views about Western society and believes women are inferior and should be subservient to men would have a hard job convincing us that they could be non-discriminatory in their practice. A black or Asian worker who hates or dislikes white people or a white worker that hates or dislikes black and Asian people could not possibly claim they are able to separate their personal, political beliefs from their professional. Despite the patchwork of ideas that informs it, anti-discriminatory practice does have a political, ethical and philosophical foundation. It is rooted in social and political struggles and it is built on values that have humanity at its core. As we have tried to highlight in this chapter, the theories that inform Anti-discriminatory practice straddle different discourses and disciplines, and include political theory, philosophy, economics, anthropology, sociology and psychology.

Points to ponder

- Is it possible that an individual's action/practice can be separated from their views, beliefs and values?
- How important is self-reflection and awareness in developing an anti-discriminatory approach?
- How useful or relevant are socio-cultural discourses in helping us get a better understanding of anti-discriminatory practice? Do they help us shed any light on the concept and implementation?
- Is anti-discriminatory practice capable of addressing different and competing voices and needs?
- Should anti-discriminatory practice be considered a universal concept or should it be regarded purely in relativistic terms?
- Is it possible to sustain the view that not all forms of discrimination are wrong and unacceptable and still believe in anti-discriminatory practice?

3

Models of Anti-discriminatory Practice

Introduction
Person-centred approach
Key concepts
Attitudinal and behavioural approaches
Structural considerations
A separate approach
Integrated services
Empowerment
Conclusion

models of ADP

INTRODUCTION

The focus of this chapter is, firstly, to describe the historical context of anti-discriminatory practice and, secondly, to discuss the range of strategies that have been adopted over the years to deal with it. According to Dominelli (2004), the commitment to anti-oppressive, hence anti-discriminatory practice, has a long history in the social work profession. In her view, anti-discriminatory practice is thought of as being of equal importance alongside the knowledge that social workers are expected to acquire and the skills that are required for the task of social work.

The social work profession likes to link its history to the early charitable organisations, parish relief and philanthropists who provided help and support to the poor and the destitute, but of course shies away from associating itself with the Poor Law Relief Act 1834 and the workhouse regimes. In reality, however, the poor law and the workhouse, although the conditions were harsh and inhumane, were the precursors to the development of state welfare provision. The social work profession now views itself as a caring profession that attempts to make a difference in

37

people's lives by providing a stable environment from which people can begin to rebuild their lives.

Historically, the profession's valorisation of respect for the individual has its foundations in religious doctrines and was later formulated into the guiding set of principles (values) articulated by Biestek in the 1960s. As Dominelli (2004: 64) highlighted, 'Biestek (1961) identified and propounded the values of social work as: individualisation; the purposeful expression of feelings; controlled emotional involvement; acceptance; a non-judgemental attitude; client self-determination; and confidentiality'. In many respects, Biestek's ideas could be regarded as the early tentative building blocks of anti-discriminatory practice because at the heart of these concepts was the call for an approach that encouraged self-awareness and the need for practitioners to recognise the impact of prejudice on people's lives. He recognised the importance of treating people as unique individuals and that they should be accepted for who they are rather than what they may represent. In other words, people should be approached from a non-judgemental perspective and they should be treated with dignity and respect. Quite far-sighted in many ways, it encouraged an approach that saw people not as mere puppets but 'actors' who are capable of self-determination.

The values that Biestek expounded have had a major influence in social work education and in practice because they underpin all aspects of the profession's approach. The fact that Biestek's ideas emerged in the late 1950s and early 1960s was not surprising since the period was characterised by internal political upheavals, global economic development and geo-political realignments. It was a time when there was a clamour for social and political equality throughout the world. It was during the period when many countries that were under colonial subjugation fought and gained their independence. Events that were taking place in one continent affected social relationships and political enfranchisement in another. For example, although the civil rights movement originated in the United States of America, its impact reverberated in Africa, Asia, Europe, Central and South America. The demand for justice, equality and fairness by the civil rights campaigners were sentiments that were well understood by people in other countries.

As a profession that saw itself as the champion of the poor, the dispossessed and those who are marginalised, it was not surprising to find social work embracing the call for social justice and placing itself at the vanguard of calling for non-discriminating welfare provision. From its inception, social work has always viewed itself as a profession that is

more interested in caring for people and providing help and support in a way that is non-stigmatising and is sensitive to the needs of those who are recipients of services. The issue was how to strike the right balance between a sensitive and non-stigmatising service on the one hand and on the other ensuring that people who are in need get the service they required. This was not an easy task. The difficulty was the inextricable linking of welfare provision and stigma in the eyes of both the general public and the recipients of welfare. As Plant, Lesser and Taylor-Gooby recognised, 'The concept of need is also crucial to the social services in that the relationship between needs and rights lies at the heart of the problem of stigma and social service provision' (1980: 22).
They continued:

> In the context of the recipients of social services, the term (stigma) is used to indicate that such recipients feel that they are receiving charity or some kind of handout from the state when their needs are being met, rather than feeling that they are receiving some benefit to which they have a moral, as opposed to positive, legal entitlement, something to which they have a right. (1980: 23)

We would argue that keeping it 'real' and being focused on service users and understanding the nature of discrimination underlined the equality debates in the 1960s, 1970s and early part of the 1980s. It also impacted on wider, heated discussions about the scope and nature of social work practice and social welfare provisions (Smalley 1970; Titmus 1976; Pinker 1979; Corden and Preston-Shoot 1987). However, the interesting point was that while social work was at the forefront of campaigning for equality for all, there were many individuals and groups who were complaining about the level of discrimination in social work, both in terms of the difficulties people had in accessing services and in the way the services were provided by social workers (Gilroy 1987; Dominelli 1988; Barnes and Mercer 2003). For example, some authors looked at the experiences of black children in the public care system and expressed their concerns about the lack of knowledge about how to care for the children adequately or any understanding of minority children and their families (Ahmed, Cheetham and Small 1986; Dominelli 1988; Barn 1993) while others highlighted the general lack of recognition, by social work professionals, of lesbian and gay issues and the inadequate and sexist approach towards women service users (Schoenberg, Goldberg and Shore 1985; Brown 1992; Langan and Day 1992; Williams 1992).

THE PERSON-CENTRED APPROACH

Having highlighted the paradox that existed between the aims and aspirations embodied in social work values and the discriminatory practices that existed in reality, we must note, however, that within the profession there was recognition and acceptance that things needed to change. Societal influences on the profession in the 1960s, 1970s and 1980s was evident in the calls for equal rights and treatment for women, lesbians and gay people, black people, including other minority groups and people with impairments as well as working-class people. There was a real sense during these turbulent times that anything was possible and, in particular, that structures and systems could be developed that could transform the lives of those in need. It was during this period, we would argue, that social work began to look at itself in a more critical way and to explore ways in which the profession could best address how it related to those who were users of social services. It was during the same period that the works of Biestek (1961) and Carl Rogers (1951 and 1961) came into sharp focus because their ideas encouraged practitioners to recognise the importance of treating people as human beings and understanding their experiences and the difficulties they faced in their lives. There was great emphasis on social workers being non-judgemental, encouraging self-determination, maintaining confidentiality, being empathetic and working from a perspective that is based on unconditional positive regard (Trevithick 2000; Payne 2005).

Although it was never conceived as such, this was an attempt to connect the worker to the personal and social realities of service users' lives. It not only encouraged workers to understand the experiences of service users in general terms but it demanded that they vicariously enter into the service users' world and try to experience both what they see and what they feel. What has been interesting, though, has been the use of Biestek's and Rogers' ideas by social workers to serve as a proxy for an anti-discriminatory practice approach. The rationale being that the ethos, values and attitudes that are embedded in the approach encourage workers to be humane, understanding and non-discriminatory in the way they work with people. This, in essence, can be the only way of reading Biestek's notion of individualisation, because he asserted:

> Individualization is the recognition and understanding of each client's unique qualities and differential use of principles and methods in assisting each towards a better adjustment. Individualization is based upon the right of

human beings to be individuals and to be treated not just as *a* human being but as *this* human being with his personal differences. (Biestek 1961: 25)

At some level, it could be suggested that both anti-discriminatory practice and the person-centred approach are essentially the same thing and that the differences are more about terminology than substance. Although there is some truth in the assertion, we would argue, however, that there is a great deal of difference between the two approaches. The person-centred approach is characterised by:

- a non-judgemental attitude
- unconditional positive regard
- empathic understanding
- genuineness
- trust
- confidentiality
- active listening.

These characteristics described above are essentially about the nature of the dyadic relationship between the worker and the service user. They are the micro-skills required for effective work with individual clients and service users. This theoretical and philosophical perspective suggests that people are neither objects nor mere puppets to be manipulated by workers. Instead, workers have to act professionally and owe a duty of responsibility and care towards services users. The approach envisages that workers have the capacity to listen and be capable of purging themselves of negative attitudes in order to demonstrate respect towards service users. One of the unique aspects of the approach is that it is a transforming doctrine and individuals are expected to reconsider their values and temper their attitudes and behaviour accordingly. Its foundation (also one of the criticisms) lies in the belief that to make a difference one has to focus on the interaction between the worker and the service user. In other words, prejudices, negative attitudes and lack of understanding about the experiences of others happen when the worker distances themselves from and are not *there* with the person they are purporting to help.

There are many criticisms that could be levelled against the person-centred approach and one indeed has already been mentioned. It could be suggested that it is paternalistic in its view towards service users as it fails to recognise the power differential between the worker and the service user by focusing only on the change that would occur as a result of the relationship between them. Unlike anti-discriminatory practice, which operates both at the micro and the macro levels, it fails to acknowledge the importance of identity, power, culture, systems, structures and processes both at the social and at the organisational level. However, it is worth acknowledging that the General Social Care Council has incorporated, in its Codes of Practice for all social care workers, Biestek and Rogers' ideas. The Codes of Practice for social care workers, which consist of six sections (there are also five sections that relate to employers), set out unambiguously the standards of practice and the standards of conduct within which they are expected to work. In essence, a breach of any aspect of the Codes could result in disciplinary proceedings. For our purpose, it is in section 1: 'As a social worker, you must protect the rights and promote the interests of service users and carers', and section 5: 'As a social care worker, you must uphold public trust and confidence in social care services' (GSCC – codes of practice) that issues relating to anti-discrimination practice are located.

This is by no means an exhaustive overview of the background to the development of anti-discriminatory strategies but rather it serves to contextualise the discussion about anti-discriminatory practice, and to suggest that although social work values are imbued with care, sensitivity and non-judgemental attitudes, in reality the high ideals that characterised the culture and ethos of the profession have not always been demonstrated in practice.

KEY CONCEPTS

As a result of the recognition that society is characterised by discrimination and inequality and that some people face discrimination and unfair treatment because of their gender, social class, religious beliefs, sexual orientation, impairment, ethnicity and because of their colour, there was a genuine attempt by the social work profession to try and tackle the problem. Over the years, there have been a number of strategies that have been developed and adopted to tackle discriminatory practices – these include approaches that focused on practitioners' *attitudes and behaviour*; those that concentrated on the systems and structures; there were suggestions by some for a *separatist approach* and others who advocated a more *integrated service*, while yet others advocated an *empowerment* and user involvement approach. Finally, many practitioners rely on the principle values of social work that were developed by Biestek and

Rogers' person-centred approach as their mainstay for ensuring that their approaches and practices do not oppress or discriminate.

To a large extent, we would argue that these are the fault lines along which the discussions about how best to tackle discriminatory practices are drawn. Although there are fundamental differences between the strategies, there are some overlaps between them. It is not unusual for different strategies to be employed at the same time.

ATTITUDINAL AND BEHAVIOURAL APPROACHES

Historically, it can be shown that in the 1970s and 1980s, social work, alongside education, were the professions at the forefront of attempting to tackle discriminatory practices not just within their respective professions but in society at large. The initial attempt to tackle discriminatory practices focused on practitioners' prejudices and their attitudes. There was a belief that unless people were made to look at themselves and compelled to examine their negative attitudes and prejudices towards others, then discrimination would continue to be perpetuated both personally and professionally. Influenced perhaps by the teachings in behavioural psychology, especially the aspects that explored primary and secondary socialisation influences (Miller 1987; Milner 1993; Millam 2002), great emphasis was placed on the development of people's perceptions and the ideas found in perceptual-accentuation and perceptual-defence (Medcof and Roth 1979). Many of the early attempts to tackle discrimination within the social work profession, such as Racism Awareness Training (RAT), and Sexism Awareness Training (SAT), focused exclusively on getting individuals to look at their attitudes and beliefs and the extent to which they both personally and as members of a dominant group benefited from the prevailing arrangements.

There was an underlying assumption that, whether by acts of omission or commission, the mere fact of being a member of the group deemed to be the oppressors makes all members of that group oppressors. To illustrate the point, Miles (1990) highlighted Katz's argument and observed that:

> second, this concept of racism is ultimately teleological. If, as Katz argues, racism is a disease that all 'white' people 'have', and if racism is 'perpetuated by whites through their conscious and/or unconscious support of a culture and institutions that are founded on racist policies and practices'

(1978: 10), then all 'white' actions (and inactions) are racist. The definition is all-inclusive, with the result that, for example, if a 'white' person suggests that because, by definitions, all 'whites' and all acts which sustain the status quo are racist and all 'whites' are sick. (Miles 1990: 56)

Although Miles' example relates to racism, the same assertion could be extrapolated to other groups outside the mainstream or those who experience oppressive and discriminatory practices. The outcome was that training programmes were devised to encourage people to first of all acknowledge their 'inherent' propensity for oppressing and discriminating against others. Once there was an acknowledgement and acceptance of their culpability, they then needed to purge themselves of the values, beliefs and attitudes that had enabled them to perpetuate discriminatory practices. As Millam (2002) acknowledged, looking at the subjects of race, class, gender, sexual orientation, impairment and ageism within the context of discrimination is not easy and having to explore them in an open forum, where those who believed themselves to be victims of discrimination are sitting across the room from those who were seen as the oppressors, was bound to be fraught with problems. The emotional turmoil that was unleashed made it very difficult for people to speak openly and to look at the subject in a positive way. Rather than tackling discrimination at its core, there was acrimony, anger and polarisation between individuals and groups. During the training sessions, there was a great deal of pain and hurt expressed by some and people who were accused of being oppressors felt victimised, oppressed and discriminated against by those who were themselves victims of discriminatory practices.

Not all such programmes were negative – a great deal depended on the sensitivity and the group facilitating skills of the trainer(s) involved. To be successful, the facilitator(s) had to be free of their own prejudices and work from a premise that no group or individual has a monopoly on discrimination and that there is no hierarchy of oppression. In addition, they would need to demonstrate the ability to 'hold' the group together and support individuals while uncomfortable and painful experiences are expressed openly.

Far from tackling discrimination as intended, awareness training programmes became in danger of entrenching people's positions because of its essentialist and deterministic underlying principle. In time, there came the backlash against this over concentration on people's attitudes.

There was a questioning of the value of looking at attitudes when really the focus should be on people's behaviour and their actions. The rationale was that people could hold whatever view they liked as long as they did not allow it to interfere with their duties and responsibilities of providing an equal and non-discriminatory service to all.

One of the interesting points to note is that during this period when there was a great emphasis placed on attitudes and behaviours, there was already legislation in place that recognised the importance of tackling discriminatory practices by looking both at individuals and organisations (structures) and setting out what was legally acceptable. For example, there was the Chronically Sick and Disabled Act 1970; the 1975 Equal Pay Act, which set out clearly that there should be no differentiation in pay between women and men who were doing the same or a comparable job; the 1975 Sex Discrimination Act which stipulates that men and women must not suffer discrimination on the grounds of their sex; the 1976 Race Relations Act which defines four different kinds of discrimination (direct, indirect, segregation and victimization); and the 1988 Education Reform Act which championed the promotion of the spiritual, moral, cultural, mental and physical development of children in school and society. To some extent, this legislative and policy framework acted as an important bridge into the next phase of practices and thinking for tackling discriminatory practices (see Chapter 5 for discussion about relevant legislation and the full range of anti-discriminatory policies).

STRUCTURAL CONSIDERATIONS

In her work on the subject of racism in social work, Dominelli challenged the notion that because social work values encourage a non-judgemental attitude towards others, it is therefore immune from discriminatory practices. In her view:

> White social workers' fond belief in their liberalism and non-judgemental openness is endorsed in a study by Bagley and Young (1982). This suggests social workers are more 'racially tolerant' than the general populace because only 3 per cent of them are racialist, i.e., hold crude racist views, compared to 20 per cent of the population as a whole. By identifying racism primarily in its overt forms, this definition of racism endorses its manifestation as the preserve of fanatical right-wing movements, groups and individuals. (1988: 21)

She cautioned against individualising discrimination by suggesting:

> Making racism in social work practice a matter of individual import ignores the role of institutionalised racism and discounts the significance of direct or unintentional racism. It pathologises the overtly racist few, ignores the subtle racism of the majority, and obscures the interconnections between structural forces and personal behaviour. Moreover, it converts racism into a matter which can be educated away, thereby ignoring the link between its eradication and the transformation of our socio-economic and political structures. (ibid.)

She continues her analysis thus:

> And because only a 'few' white social workers are considered racist, it condones the belief that anti-racist struggles are activities which white social workers undertake either as an educational exercise aimed at promoting understanding of other people and their cultures, or as political activities undertaken outside working hours. (ibid.)

The concerns expressed by Dominelli (1988) were that it would be a mistake to believe that only a small number of social workers were, in this case, racist and that rather than focus attention only on this small number, the profession needed to look at its practice as a whole. It needed to question the approach of locating all the inequalities and discriminations that people experience on the shoulders of individuals. Such a starting point takes little or no account of the role that organisational and societal structures, cultures and systems play in the maintenance and perpetuation of discrimination. According to Vivian and Brown (1995) and Thompson (2003a), whose observations are still of relevance, an over-reliance on personality-based understanding of discrimination misses the point because there are broader socio-structural dimensions that also need to be put into the mix.

As Thompson observed:

> A reliance on personal explanation of discrimination is problematic ... In order to go beyond the personal level, we need to consider the cultural context in which individuals operate. Although each individual is to some extent unique, we also have to recognise that individual beliefs, values and actions owe a great deal to prevailing norms and expectations. (2003a: 14)

The recognition that there are many factors external to the individual that needed to be taken into consideration in tackling discrimination was important because it allowed for the shifting of emphasis to include structures, systems and processes. This was a significant turning point in the thinking of the profession.

A SEPARATE APPROACH

Periodically, there is a call by activists and some commentators for an approach that is akin to separatist provision. Although, at some level, it could be argued that the division of services into adults, children and families, disability and mental health is a kind of separatist provision, in fact the difference is that the specialism relates to the services that are being provided rather than to the recipients of the services. In other words, irrespective of a service user's race, gender, sexual orientation or religious beliefs, once they meet the necessary criteria, they would be entitled to all of the services that are available. A separatist service provision approach looks beyond the provision and services and instead focuses on the recipients. The rationale for such thinking is that as society is characterised by self-interests and that certain groups appear to dominate the political, social and cultural landscape, it is unlikely that minority groups, and others outside the mainstream, would be given the opportunity for a fair and equal access to services. Moreover, because of their unequal status and position in society, they are vulnerable to receiving a poor quality of service and are likely to experience oppressive and discriminatory practices.

For example, reference is often made to the 'experience' of the oppressed and discriminated-against groups. The 'experience' denotes the fact that because of their race, gender, impairment, sexual orientation and social class, people are liable and subjected to the critical gaze of others. In order to survive the approbation and cope with the negative projections and the stereotypical assumptions they encounter in their daily lives, people have had to devise coping strategies. The view is that in order for people to have equal access to services and be treated fairly and with dignity and respect, then those organising, providing and managing the provisions not only have to be sympathetic to people's 'experience' but they have to be from the same group and, preferably, have had the same 'experience'. According to this approach, the only way to eliminate oppressive and discriminatory practices is by ensuring that people who organise, provide and manage the service are the same as or have had the same experiences as those who are the recipients of the service. In this case, men would not be involved in providing services for women, those with impairments would be dealt with by people with impairments and minority groups would be dealt with only by people from the same ethnic group, etc.

Although there has been some flexibility in that some organisations have made it possible that in certain circumstances a services user could request that they be dealt with by a worker who is of the same gender or cultural background, in most instances the opportunity is not extended to all. In many respects, the separatist approach for dealing with oppressive and discriminatory practices has not been officially adopted. Of course, there are many private and voluntary organisations that provide a range of services that are targeted at particular groups. For example, there are housing organisations, community organisations, clinics and social welfare groups, but these are exceptions rather than the rule and they are generally not part of the mainstream services. Aside from political and ideological explanations, one of the reasons why the separatist approach has not taken root, we would argue, owes more to the problem of attracting finance and the logistical and practical difficulty of applying it.

INTEGRATED SERVICES

While there are ideological and practical difficulties for not adopting the separatist approach, more specifically we would argue that there was a genuine belief that the only way to combat oppressive and discriminatory practices was to provide an integrative service. In other words, there was an assumption that it was only by working together and living alongside each other that people, irrespective of their backgrounds and differences, would be able to develop both a better understanding of others and appreciate the reality of each other's experiences. So in this case, rather than familiarity breeding contempt, it would instead generate a more informed knowledge and understanding of the 'other'. The forces behind this assumption were partly fuelled by the knowledge, based on experience, that as people live and work amongst each other and as they are exposed to each other's daily lives, then it was more likely that any social and communication barriers would ultimately be removed. In essence, social and geographical connections are expected to play a major role in dispelling and demystifying the myths that have developed about the 'other'. An integrative service was as much about expanding the diversity of the workforce to reflect the community as it was about ensuring that services were made accessible to all. Although on the surface the integrative approach would seem the best way to combat oppressive and discriminatory practices, in reality allowances had to be made for differences, either because of religious sensitivities, cultural differences and/or as result of gender considerations. The integrative approach could be mistakenly or unfairly denounced as a 'tabula rasa' (blank slate) approach because it concentrates on ensuring that service provisions are about meeting people's needs irrespective of their biography and backgrounds. It is an approach that sees the person and treats everybody the same irrespective of their affiliations or background. It works on the premise that if people's backgrounds, appearances and characteristics were not accentuated, then it is more likely to be the case that the focus of the interaction would be on the presenting problems and the interventions rather than who they were. The critics of this approach may suggest that the very premise upon which the approach is based is both naïve and flawed because it assumes everyone can be treated the same. For the critics, it is important to recognise that while people are unique in their own right and should be treated accordingly, they are also members of groups and communities and therefore do not exist in a vacuum. In our view, to deal with people without taking account of both the historical legacies and the societal context in which they exist, with all its machinations, would be to ignore important influences that contribute towards shaping people's lives and experiences.

EMPOWERMENT

It was not until the early 1990s that the term empowerment gained momentum and became a catch-all term that denoted a way of working that was non-discriminatory. Although it was never billed as such, it was clear, in our view, that empowerment was a strategy for tackling oppressive and discriminatory practices. At a basic level, the rationale of empowerment is that in any encounter or interaction that takes place, there are underlying power imbalances between the people involved. For the practitioner not to be oppressive or discriminatory in their approach, they have to become an enabler and facilitator with the responsibility of shifting the power imbalance between themselves and the service user. In other words, rather than treating the individual or groups as mere passive recipients of services, their knowledge and understanding should be the basis upon which any intervention is based. Empowerment could, at some level, be characterised as a way of helping people to help themselves by promoting and facilitating their independence and providing them with the 'key' (or social capital) that would enable them to conduct their affairs without social work involvement.

CONCLUSION

Although anti-discriminatory practice is the umbrella term that is used to tackle discrimination and discriminatory practices, the model or approach that is adopted by institutions and organisations very much depends on their ethos and philosophical standpoint. What we have tried to demonstrate in this chapter is that there is tension between approaches that encourage an inclusive approach and those that sepa-ratist in orientation, and, between those that are service focused and those that are service-user focused. Some organisations of course strad-dle both camps while others, for good reasons, adopt a service-user bias. For example, there are black and Asian organisations that not only have black and Asian service users but all their staff are also from the same group. Similarly, there are some services that are exclusively for women and others which target gay men and lesbians and again they are staffed by people from those communities. Despite the fact that this category of service is exclusively focused on a particular community, it would be difficult to label them as separatist. The reason they are not separatist is because they are not driven or motivated by politics and ideology but rather by safety (women), or pragmatic and safety (gay men, lesbians, black and Asian service users) reasons. In the main, the aim of these areas of service provision is often to look towards re-establishing people back into mainstream services. One of the key aspects that has already been highlighted in this chapter is the fact that anti-discriminatory practice is not a new concept in social work. It is evident that contained within the body of social work, in particular the client-centred approach, are principles and values that form the important foundation for developing anti-discriminatory practice. The criticism has been and continues to be that they are too focused on individual practitioners' actions and beliefs and fail to take account of the wider systemic and socio-structural influences.

Points to ponder

- Is there much difference between anti-discriminatory practice and the person-centred approach?
- Is it fair to suggest that anti-discriminatory practice does not adequately take account of difference but views all forms of discrimination in the same way?
- Does the mere fact of being a member of a group identified as the oppressors mean all members of that group oppress others? For example, are all men sexist? Are all white people racist? Are all people without disability oppressors of people with impairment?
- Are some groups/individuals more oppressed and discriminated against than others?
- If it is accepted that there is a hierarchy of oppression and discrimination, what would it look like?
- Would a separatist service provision approach address the problem of discrimination in social welfare services?

models of ADP

4
The Political Dimension of Anti-discriminatory Practice

> *Introduction*
> *The political nature of anti-discriminatory practice*
> *The de-coupling of politics: Thatchblairist ideology*
> *Key concepts*
> *The political act of challenging*
> *Conclusion*

INTRODUCTION

This chapter explores the political dimension of anti-discriminatory practice and highlights the fact that anti-discriminatory practice was borne out of the political struggles of the 1960s and 1980s. It suggests that while it is understandable that cultural and sexual politics should be placed at the centre of anti-discriminatory practice, it would be a mistake to disentangle the concept from its political pedigree. In the 1980s, anti-discriminatory practice's primary focus on race and gender was unfortunate because there was a sense of disassociation between other discriminations and race and gender. Although a great deal of work has been done to integrate other areas of discrimination into the main body of anti-discriminatory practice, there are still attempts to view and approach all discriminations as if they exist in discreet 'silos'. This is not to reintroduce the mixed salad or melting pot notion but it is to suggest that to ignore or play down all other discrimination would do a great disservice to the ethos and aims of anti-discriminatory practice. In addition, we are particularly keen to reinsert politics back into anti-discriminatory practice because it would be illogical not to do so. In our view, some of the key concepts that contribute to the development of anti-discriminatory practice are political in nature. One of the most intriguing observations when looking at current approaches towards anti-discriminatory practice is the way it has, somehow, become de-coupled from its political roots. To understand how this de-coupling occurred, a brief discussion of the development of the concept and the complex and dynamic environment in which it operates may prove useful.

It is no longer uncommon to read a great deal of criticism about the legacy of the 1960s and how, while ushering in a new society with greater social, economic, political and sexual freedom, it also brought in its wake unforeseen consequences. One of the charges is that the period was instrumental in dismantling structures and systems that fostered family and social cohesion and people's sense of duty to society and responsibility for others. But it is worth acknowledging that for many decades the 1960s was a period lauded by commentators, opinion formers and academics as a defining period in the evolution of social, political and personal emancipation. Indeed, as Thompson highlighted:

> it was a decade characterised by notions of consciousness raising in terms of both increased political radicalism and the emerging psychedelic drug culture. The radicalism was particularly apparent in the latter part of the sixties, as evidenced by student protest, occupations and so on. It was a time of idealism and anti-establishment challenge of the status quo. This was accompanied by an increased emphasis on humanitarian values and liberation. It was a time in which progressive movements flourished and the breaking down of traditional barriers was being pursued on a large scale. (2006: 3)

Similarly, in many ways, the 1960s was a defining period for social work in its attempt to develop a set of values and forge a path for itself as a profession. During that period, there was an internal struggle between those in the profession who favoured an approach that was heavily influenced by psychology (*people* in society), and those inclined towards a more sociological perspective (people in *society*). Of course, there were ideas that attempted to bridge the gap between these two different perspectives and the psycho-social model developed by Florence Hollis is perhaps the best example of this approach. Although it is no longer such a prominent method in social work practice (while the approach may still be in evidence in some corners of social work, generally, it has lost its prominence in comparison to other approaches and perspectives), it is nevertheless worth recalling that for a considerable period during the 1970s and the early part of the 1980s, Florence Hollis' approach was one of the methods which dominated

the political dimension

53

both social work education and practice. However, in the main, although social work and social workers were involved in the liberation struggle in society, the practice of social work itself was dominated and heavily influenced by psychology and, in particular, psychoanalytical/psychodynamic thinking.

As Rojek, Peacock and Collins observed:

> The deep influence of psychoanalytical thought with a focus on the relationship to the external world and the ego reactions to the drives of the id and the demands of the superego. Psychoanalytical ideas were seen as the only effective method of altering personality structure; and insight at that time was seen as the primary goal and major strategy of intervention. (1988: 21)

What is worth acknowledging is that whatever the dominant approach, there was little doubt that throughout, the aim and task of social work has remained constant and consistent. Social work has always been in the change business. It's a profession that strives to bring about change in people's circumstances and improve their life chances. It was believed that *change* was only possible by developing a better understanding of the individual's biography and looking at their intra-psychic processes and interpreting the nature of the individual's relationships with their familial environment. Change is more likely to occur when people have developed an insight about themselves. The self-awareness and the development of insight would, in turn, enable them to have a better understanding of their problems, relationship and their circumstances. Although the 1960s ushered in major social and political changes in society, somehow social work practice was more influenced by practice approaches that emphasised the importance of individual psychic and their inter- and intra-personal relationships rather than a socio-political and community-orientated approach. As Thompson highlighted, 'A similar process of consciousness raising also occurred in the UK, although again there is little evidence of the impact of this on social work' (2006: 3).

Although social work practice was dominated by psychoanalytical thinking in the 1960s and 1970s, the ethos and values that characterised the profession were actually informed by humanitarian and liberal political ideas. This was not surprising given the history and development of the profession. Anti-discriminatory practice was borne out of the political discourse that took place in the 1960s, but it is our contention that it was stripped of its political edge in the way it was implemented in the

1980s. To a large extent, the 1980s was a period of social and political fragmentation and fissure. The explanations for the massive upheaval that occurred during the period have been commendably explored by Lymbery and Butler (2004). It is quite difficult to understand why Antidiscriminatory practice took the non-political path given the volatile political climate, social unrests and economic uncertainties of the period.

The de-coupling of politics from anti-discriminatory practice is quite a major feat since anti-discriminatory practice is not just about identity and cultural politics but also about human rights and political representation, economic fairness as well as social justice and equality of opportunities for all. To think about anti-discriminatory practice without reference to or any consideration of its political history should be considered, at best, paradoxical and, at worst, illogical. The approach is and has always been about both the nature of the relationship that existed between people in society and about how the political system and social structures contribute towards discrimination and reinforce existing inequalities.

THE POLITICAL NATURE OF ANTI-DISCRIMINATORY PRACTICE

It is important to remember that anti-discriminatory practice was developed, in essence, as a counter-measure to challenge the unfair treatment that was prevalent. Also, there was a recognition that because of socially constructed demarcations and stratifications, there was a lack of equality and opportunities for many groups in society. Social work was especially sensitive to the vast range of inequalities and deprivation that existed in society because the profession was in direct contact with people that were greatly affected by it. Despite the fact that many social workers generally worked for the state, there were still heated ideological debates within the profession about their role in society and whose interests they should be serving.

As a reaction against what they saw around them, a group of radical social workers formed a group called Case Con. The group believed it was their duty to highlight the struggles of the profession and the realities of their 'clients'. They lambasted the fact that:

> Every day of the week, every week of the year, social workers (including probation officers, educational social workers, hospital social workers, community workers and local authority social workers) see the utter failure of social work to meet the real needs of the people it purports to help. (Case Con Manifesto 1970: 1)

Case Con saw itself as:

> an organisation of social workers (in the broadest sense), attempting to give an answer to the contradictions that we face. Case Con offers no magic solutions, no way in which you can go to work tomorrow and practice some miraculous new form of social work which does meet the needs of your 'clients'. It would be nice if there were such an easy answer, but we believe that the problems and frustrations we face daily are inextricably linked to the society we live in, and that we can only understand what needs to be done if we understand how the welfare state, of which social services are a part, has developed, and what pressures it is subject to. (Case Con Manifesto 1970: 1)

During the formation of Case Con, social work practice and the general approach in the profession were still dominated by the psychoanalytical/psychodynamic perspectives. However, the presence of Case Con (and others that were not so well known) attest to the fact that there was a politically driven wing within the profession that rejected the non-political approach. They believed that the focus on people's early childhood experiences as a means of understanding their problems missed the point. For them, people were products of their social environment and the political system under which they lived their lives. The prominent view of Case Con was that:

> One important tool of professional social work has been case work – a pseudo science – that blames individual inadequacies for poverty and so mystifies and diverts attention from the real causes – slums, homelessness and economic exploitation. The casework ideology forces clients to be seen as needing to change to fit society. (Case Con Manifesto 1970: 1)

Influenced by the work of Marx, Webber and the Frankfurt school, the approach also embraced the ideas of a range of feminists (black and white) and learnt from the black civil rights movement in America as well as liberation movements from Central America, Africa and Southern Asia. They wanted to challenge the dominance of the psycho-analytical approach and lay bare its contradictions and irrelevance as a way of working with poor and disadvantaged groups. Interestingly, the 1980s and 1990s saw a synergy of psychoanalytic thinking and radical left politics, as exemplified by the works and publications of the *Journal of Groups of Psychodynamic and Psychotherapy Social Work* (GAPS). However, before the thaw in relations between the radical left and the psychoanalytic group, there were fierce debates about how social work should respond to working with service users (clients). The birth of radical social work was highly significant for the profession (Bailey and Brake 1975). For example, the radical movement not only challenged the kind of approach that should be adopted in practice, it also shattered the assumption that social work should only focus on their clients (service users) and not meddle in politics. Radical social work encouraged practitioners to pay greater attention to the social environments and the social realities of their clients. So areas that were previously deemed irrelevant for social work to be involved in were now considered legitimate areas of interest because of their impact on people. As the movement gained confidence in its belief that social work had a moral duty and obligation to address the underlining social causes of their clients' predicaments, they expanded their sphere of interest. As Thompson rightly observed:

> The radical social work movement in the 1960s and 1970s raised awareness of the significance of poverty and deprivation, and drew attention to the ways in which class-based inequalities underpinned the life context of so many recipients of social work services and intervention. The 1980s saw a greater awareness of, and emphasis upon, inequalities based on gender and race or ethnicity. (2000: 12)

It was also in the 1970s and 1980s that radical social work reinforced its political edge through the incorporation of community work into the profession. There is also anecdotal evidence that many of the people who entered the social work profession during the period were idealised middle-class white women and men (freshly minted graduates from polytechnics and red-brick universities), who wanted to change the world through the social work profession. Despite the poor pay and lack of recognised professional status, many of these people were drawn to the profession because they believed they could make a difference and, more importantly, they could contribute to a better society. They were driven by the desire to help to transform the lives of those that were disadvantaged by discrimination, unfairness and injustices. They were galvanised into action because they were against a social and political system that they believed was unfair and unjust and perpetuated inequalities. Payne (1997) helpfully divided social work theories and models into three categories: reflexive-therapeutic, socialist-collectivist and individual-reformist. Many of those who were drawn to social work during the period would be classified as being inclined towards the socialist-collectivist strand. Interestingly, the practice approach and the outlook of the profession itself leant more towards the reflexive-therapeutic end.

THE DE-COUPLING OF POLITICS: THATCHBLAIRIST IDEOLOGY

There are a number of possible explanations for the de-coupling of politics from anti-discriminatory practice. One explanation could be that during the 1980s when there was great financial pressure on social service departments, there was a tendency to focus attention on the minutiae of day-to-day practice. This *managerialism* approach (as it came to be so named) paid closer attention to outcomes and how social work and social workers carry out their duties and responsibilities rather than taking account of the broader perspective. There was greater emphasis on the policing of practitioners' movements and the requirement that they justify their role and involvement in cases. There was also the streamlining of services through reorganisations of departments and services. For many practitioners, the motivating factor for re-organisations was not necessarily to improve services but to cut costs and therefore save money. In addition, social work went through a torrid period because there were scandals of children having been abused while in the care of local authorities; vulnerable children who were already known to social services being killed by their parent/s or carers; the neglect and poor care of elderly service users; the poor level of supervision and support for people with mental health problems; and the shocking treatment in residential units of children and adults with disabilities. This catalogue of events together with uncertainties about the future of social work and concerns about job security resulted in a collapse of confidence within the profession. Rather than challenging the misrepresentations and unfair criticism of its practices, the profession and practitioners appeared to retreat inwards.

At the same time as there was contraction of staff, departmental reorganisations and reduction in the range of services on offer, there was also a call by different groups in society for a social services and social work profession that was focused and geared towards their needs. So, for example, there were concerns about the over-representation of black children in the care system (Ahmed et al. 1986; Barn 1993) and the incarceration and over-reliance on the medication of patients in psychiatric institutions; there was a call for a different approach towards disability with more emphasis on 'normalisation' ideas and the integration of people into mainstream services; and there was a general call for a caring and social model approach instead of the medical model. As the 1990s drew to a close, managerialism did not disappear but it was buttressed by the idea of a new concept that was labelled the 'Third Way' (Giddens 2002). The Third Way effectively challenged the existing cold war political ideology and attempted to do away with politicking and replace it with a Thatchblairist ideology, a kind of modern-day Butskillism. Its main argument was that rather than continuing the endless cycle of left and right debates about the economic and social programmes, the emphasis should be on amalgamating different aspects of the two main political ideologies into coherent and workable policies. The rationale was that instead of a dogmatic and ideologically based politics, the aim should be to find out what works and then implement it. The call was for a new approach that is not tied down by ideology but a pragmatic approach that is 'customer' and service-user led.

It is these chains of events, we would argue, that contributed to the de-coupling of politics from both social work and anti-discriminatory practice. Instead of the reassertion of social work's political inclination, the profession reclined into a reflective practice mode. It championed a culturally sensitive approach and user involvement and encouraged empowerment. But although it vigorously fought for the implementation of anti-discriminatory practice, it was a diluted version of the concept because it was devoid of its political framework. Couldshed and Orme exemplified the apolitical approach taken by the profession. They suggested that:

> Professional social work requires that workers deploy a wide-ranging repertoire of skills, underpinned by a value base that respects others. This will enable them to respond to the diversity of experiences and reactions that are encountered when working with fellow human beings. (2006: 18)

Of course, it could be argued that Couldshed and Orme's assertion is taken out of context since they would be the first to suggest that politics should be an important consideration in social work practice. Others may argue the value base that unpinned social work (Banks 2001; Shardlow 2002; Beckett and Maynard, 2005) should not be read as mere good intentions and well meaning sophistry, but rather as values representing the profession's guiding light and the moral and ethical foundation upon which it was built. In other words, the nature of social

the political dimension

work values are such that they transcend the vagaries of political ideologies and party politics with its uncertainties and its wild swings from right to left back to the middle in a never ending cycle. Some of course may argue that it is impossible for social work to exist in a world that is devoid of politics, since all social work activities are defined and sanctioned by legislation, which of course are politically driven (Braye and Preston-Shoot 1998). Indeed, as Watson and West acknowledged:

> An understanding of wider political and agency issues can manifest itself in a number of ways when developing an approach in practice. Some workers would have come to the social work profession from a clearly defined political perspective while others may have entered the profession in an effort to 'do good' and perhaps transform, for the better, the lives of the people they are helping. What is clear though is that whatever their motivation for entering the profession, either driven by political or for non political humanitarian reasons they will still be influenced by the wider political climate. (2006: 13)

Watson and West are correct in their assertion that practitioners are affected by political ideas even though each practitioner's approach may or may not be influenced by their political perspectives. However, it would appear that despite the assumptions that all actions, including practice, are influenced by politics, it is then surprising that politics does not feature as much as identity and general awareness about differences in anti-discriminatory practice.

KEY CONCEPTS

One of the criticisms levelled against anti-discriminatory practice was that the approach does not draw enough distinction between different groups and that it puts everyone under the same marquee. For example, while it may be the case that some groups in society are subjected to discrimination, it would be naïve to then assume that there are similarities and commonalities between those groups. According to the rationale, each group has a unique experience that others would find difficult to understand. In other words, how could a Muslim man understand the experience of a lesbian? Or is it really possible for a white woman who experiences sexism to appreciate the nature of racism?

The need for differentiation and acceptance of the uniqueness of people's experiences contributed to the de-politicisation of anti-discriminatory practice. Rather than a collective approach that was based on respect of differences and an acknowledgement of similarities, there was a tendency to amplify the experiences of some groups at the expense of others. This approach fostered a hierarchy of oppression and mistakenly gave some groups the impression that not only were they the most oppressed in society but that they were also, as a result of their powerless position, incapable of oppressing others.

This approach further alienated many who saw anti-discriminatory ideas as not being particularly relevant or applicable to them. As a result of this fragmentation, anti-discriminatory practice became bureaucratised and viewed merely as part of a training exercise that had to be ticked off the list. In addition, the concept became barely indistinguishable from Rogers' person-centred casework. The Rogerian approach encourages a way of working that is non-directive, non-confrontational, non-judgemental, as well as accepting the person for who they were. These sentiments are not unfamiliar to anti-discriminatory practice but while the Rogerian approach focuses exclusively on the nature of the relationship between the worker and the service user, anti-discriminatory practice goes much further than that, as already discussed at greater length in this book. It is worth acknowledging that it was in an effort to inject a more critical edge to practice that the anti-oppressive approach was developed alongside anti-discriminatory practice. As Payne (2005) observed, anti-oppressive practice links itself very closely under the socialist-collectivist banner, but it is more of a value base rather than an approach per se. We would argue that to some extent anti-oppressive practice is essentially an attempt at a rebirth of anti-discriminatory practice under a different guise.

THE POLITICAL ACT OF CHALLENGING

So, what is being advanced is that anti-discriminatory practice could not have developed in a political vacuum but rather the concept was, from its inception, steeped in politics. As previously mentioned, the idea was developed as a challenge to an existing social order that not only privileged some groups over others but actively discriminated against many people in society. Anti-discriminatory practice was developed to combat discriminatory services in a society that was characterised by social and economic inequalities and reinforced by sexism, racism, homophobia, ageism and disablism, etc. In essence, anti-discriminatory practice was a direct challenge to service provision in a society where an individual's social and economic opportunities and life chances were determined by their social class, their ethnicity, their gender and the level of their impairment. Challenging the orthodoxy was and continues to be a political act that requires both direct and indirect actions involving a multitude of people from different social and racial backgrounds from across the political spectrum. At present, the social work profession continues to focus on ensuring that practitioners are fit to practice in a sensitive, appropriate and caring manner with an emphasis on a non-discriminatory and non-oppressive service provision. However, the caring manner that is encouraged coupled with the values, ethics and ethos of the profession should not be deemed incompatible with or devoid of politics.

CONCLUSION

The aim of this chapter was to provide a background discussion of the political dimension of anti-discriminatory practice. The relegation of politics to the sidelines in anti-discriminatory practice is both unfortunate and misplaced. As we have tried to demonstrate, Anti-discriminatory practice was borne out of the liberation struggle and its foundation can be found in the political struggle for social justice, class struggle and freedom and equality for all. Anti-discriminatory practice exclusively focuses on identity and diversity and contributed to the misconception that the approach was apolitical.

Points to ponder

- Could a Muslim man understand the experience of a lesbian woman? Is it really possible for a white woman who experiences sexism to appreciate the nature of racism?
- Should anti-discriminatory practice be considered as a concept that is apolitical?
- Is there any significant difference between anti-discriminatory practice and anti-oppressive practice?
- Is it the case that oppressed people in society, because of their powerless position, are incapable of oppressing others to the same degree?

5
Legislation and
Policies

INTRODUCTION

This chapter sets out the legislative framework that underpins the ideas and philosophy of anti-discriminatory practice, and how they culminate in equal opportunities policies at a local level. The aim is to provide both an historical overview of how legislation has evolved in this area, and to illustrate the difference between what is actually sanctioned by law and what has developed, increasingly, as a matter of 'culture' within the health and social care and social work field. There is often confusion between what is permissible in law and what may be deemed as the 'right thing to do'. Discussing the policy and legal framework under which anti-discriminatory practice operates is important for a number of reasons. Firstly, it serves to separate myth from reality and, hopefully, perhaps lay to rest many of the assumptions and misrepresentations that abound in this area. Secondly, it may helpfully highlight both the shortcomings and the gaps that exist within the current legal framework.

One of the criticisms levelled against health and social care professionals is that they do not necessarily have knowledge of the legal framework in which they work (Brayne and Carr 2005). For many workers in the health and social work field, anti-discriminatory practice is not considered to be a legal issue but a moral imperative and a matter of personal and professional values. But as Brayne and Carr observed:

> it is not enough to do your best to treat all people with respect and all people equally. Your own conduct and professional integrity, to put it simply, are not sufficient. You need to know the law from the principles which underpin it through to the duties which it imposes on you and others. You will be judged against the standards laid down; for some, rights are not just benchmarks but are enforceable through courts and tribunals. (2005: 33)

The point that Brayne and Carr are making is that it is not enough to have good intentions and to be non-discriminatory in one's attitude and actions, even though such attitudes and actions are directed by a range of considerations, including moral, ethical and personal values and a professional code of conduct. The aim is to have an awareness of and to understand the legal implications and limitations of anti-discriminatory practice. They urge, for example, that practitioners should have a 'working knowledge of the basic principles of the Human Rights Act 1998, the Race Relations Act 1976 (Amended 2002), the Sex Discrimination Act 1975, the Disability Discrimination Act 1995, and emerging laws relating to discrimination based on sexual orientation, gender reassignment, religion, or age' (Brayne and Carr 2005: 33).

There are a number of key legislations and regulations that are primarily concerned with unfairness, discrimination and equality issues. Despite the assumption that anti-discriminatory practice is a relatively new concept, it is interesting to note that some of the legislation has been on statute for quite some time. Listed here are the main areas of legislation and commissions that we suggest support anti-discriminatory practice:

- The Equal Pay Act 1970
- The Chronically Sick and Disabled Person Act 1970
- The Sex Discrimination Act 1975 (Public Authorities) (Statutory Duties) Order 2006
- The Race Relations Act 1976 (Amended 2002)
- The Disability Discrimination Act 1995 (Amendment Regulations 2003)
- The Disability Discrimination (Meaning of Disability) Regulations 1996

- The Human Rights Act 1998
- The Carers and Disabled Children Act 2000
- The Special Educational Needs and Disability Act 2002 (SENDA)
- The Employment Equality (Religion or Belief) Regulations 2003
- The Employment Equality (Sexual Orientation) (Amendment) Regulations 2003
- The Gender Recognition and Reassignment Act 2004
- The Disability Discrimination Act 2005
- Age Discrimination legislation (forthcoming).

In addition to the legislation, commissions were set up so that identified areas remain under constant monitoring in order to ensure compliance. These include:

- The Equal Opportunity Commission
- The Commission for Racial Equality
- The Disability Rights Commission.

The Commission for Equality and Human Rights (CEHR) has taken over the role, duties and responsibilities of the other three commissions. So, in essence, CEHR is the amalgamation of all the other commissions: Equal Opportunity; Racial Equality and Disability Rights Commission.

In addition, there are other pieces of legislation that have Anti-discriminatory elements embedded in them, for example:

- The Children Act 1989 and 2004
- The National Health and Community Care Act 1990
- The Education Act 2002
- The Mental Health Act 2007
- The Adoption and Fostering Act 2008.

These all make general reference to the need to ensure that service provision is non-discriminatory and that organisations take account of the cultural and religious background of the service users.

MYTH AND REALITY: THE DIFFERENCE BETWEEN POSITIVE DISCRIMINATION AND AFFIRMATIVE ACTION

Unsurprisingly, perhaps, there are many myths about what is permissible in law in relation to anti-discriminatory practice. One of the most widely held beliefs is that both positive discrimination and affirmative actions are permissible in law. The myth is that because of *positive discrimination*, minority groups, people with disabilities and women are given jobs or promoted to posts, to which they may or may not be qualified, in order to increase their representation in an organisation. Associated with this is the assumption that some kind of a quota system operates and that organisations are compelled to employ certain groups/individuals in order to meet the required quota and remain within the law. It is important to note that in the UK there is no quota system entrenched in any of the Acts. The nearest to a quota system is in the Chronically Sick and Disabled Person Act 1970. This Act permitted medium and large size companies and organisations to employ a certain percentage of disabled people in their organisation. Although there was provision within the law for recruiting disabled people, there is little evidence that medium or large companies or any organisations took advantage of recruiting disabled people in any numbers (although it must be acknowledged that the BBC and a number of local authorities did make greater effort in the latter half of the 1990s).

One of the explanations for the persistence of the belief that there is a quota system is that some organisations and agencies have developed rationing processes that enable them to manage the high volume of demands for their provisions and/or services. For example, some social housing organisations, in deciding how to allocate their limited housing stocks, have had to devise a process that is not only seen to be fair but also takes account of priority needs. So many of these organisations use a combined points-based system (points are awarded based on health condition, number of children in the family, social and family circumstance), as well as quotas. The quota system has just started to be used in the immigration field. Interestingly, the quota system was initiated in the USA in 1921 to limit the number of migrants entering the country. Britain and many other European countries have started using similar schemes as a means of restricting the numbers and sorts of migrants that are allowed into Europe.

While there is some evidence that a quota system is being used in a limited number of areas, this has not been sanctioned by law but rather is an administrative device developed by organisations to help them ration their limited resources. It is worth acknowledging that from the outset there is no legal basis for positively discriminating (positive discrimination) in favour of any one individual or groups over others in Britain. Within the field of anti-discriminatory practice, there are no quota systems in operation nor is there positive discrimination. Even section 5 (2) (D) of the Race Relations Act 1976, which allows for the recruitment into a post of a person from a particular racial group, is quite specific and very limited in its scope. This section of the Act only allows the recruitment of such persons in occupations where personal and welfare services are being provided and it has been deemed that a person of that racial group can most effectively provide such services. This is a long way short of a quota scheme or positive discrimination as it is often suggested.

The *affirmative action* or *positive action* is an American concept that has a specific meaning. The concept was developed in order to open up education and/or employment opportunities to certain groups or individuals who have been previously denied access. The concept was appropriated by the two main political parties in Britain (Labour and Conservatives) as a way of tackling the underrepresentation of women and people from ethnic minority backgrounds in the House of Commons (Members of Parliament). To address the underrepresentation, the two main parties discussed, within their parties, the legality of having an all female (Conservatives) shortlist and an all black and minority (Labour) list of parliamentary candidates. The legality of having such a closed list of black and women candidates is always questioned and contested by a sizeable number of Members of Parliament and a large section of the rank and file supporters of the two parties. In essence, affirmative action is one way of getting organisations and institutions to increase the representation of minorities, women and people with disability in their workforce. But it is important to make clear that at present in Britain, affirmative action or positive discrimination are not features of any legislation.

GENDER BIAS

There are two pieces of legislation relating to discrimination on the grounds of sex (gender): there is the Equal Pay Act 1970 and the Sex Discrimination Act 1975. What is often forgotten is that both Acts apply equally to both women and men. The Equal Pay Act made it unlawful to discriminate against women or men on pay. One of the criticisms against the Act is that, despite many of the successes achieved by individual litigation, it has not been effective in eliminating the pay gaps that still exist between men and women. The 'glass ceiling' is often said to denote the lack of opportunities for women to progress beyond certain positions in some fields of employment.

While the Equal Pay Act attempted to address the inequalities that exist between the pay of men and women, the Sex Discrimination Act 1975 (SDA) focused, uncompromisingly, on protecting against unlawful discrimination towards (again both) men and women. The Act makes sex discrimination unlawful in employment, vocational training, education, the provision and sale of goods, facilities and services, the management and letting of premises and in the exercise of public functions. The Sex Discrimination Act 1975 was quite progressive because it established the Equal Opportunity Commission. The commission had statutory powers to enforce both the Equal Pay Act and the Sex Discrimination Act. In fact, the commission has been active in ensuring that all subsequent gender equality legislation were kept under constant review and monitoring.

The Sexual Discrimination Act 1975 was further strengthened by (Statutory Duties) Order 2006, which placed a duty on public authorities to have due regard to the 'need to eliminate unlawful discrimination and harassment and to promote equality of opportunity between men and women'. In addition to these Acts, there are other pieces of legislation that protect people's rights towards equal pay, for example there is the European Union Law (article 141 of the treaty of Amsterdam); the Part-Time Workers Regulation 2000 (amended 2002 and 2005); and finally the Human Rights Act 1998.

Yet despite all these measures, women, in general, still face formidable obstacles in society as they attempt to establish their right to equal treatment and opportunities. It is noteworthy that both in the public and private spheres, women still experience discriminatory attitudes and practices and this despite the fact that the enactment of legal frameworks that outlawed such discriminatory practices have been in existence for well over 30 years.

THE RACE QUESTION

The Race Relations Act 1976 was, in many respects, a landmark piece of legislation that was meant to transform the nature of the relationships between people in society. This Act was not the only one that attempted to address race relations in society but was in fact a consolidating Act because it incorporated the earlier 1965 and 1968 Race Relations Acts. The Act was established to promote race equality in society and, more crucially, to prevent discrimination on the grounds of race, colour, nationality and ethnicity. It outlawed direct and indirect racial discrimination in the fields of employment, education and housing and in the provision of goods, services and facilities. The Act acknowledged the multifaceted nature of discrimination by recognising and highlighting the differences between direct (overt) discrimination and indirect (covert) discrimination. One of the myths about this Act is that it only applies to black people. In fact, the Act applies to everyone in society because it takes account of and is concerned with race as well as nationality and ethnicity. So non-black people, for example 'travellers' and white individuals, have been able to successfully challenge discrimination using aspects of the Race Relations Act to support their case.

The Race Relations Act 1976 was a transforming act because it also established the Commission for Racial Equality (CRE), effectively a monitoring and policing organisation whose tasks it was:

- to encourage greater integration and better relations between people from different ethnic groups
- to use its legal powers to help eradicate racial discrimination and harassment
- to work with government and public authorities to promote racial equality in all public services
- to support local and regional organisations, and employers in all sectors, in their efforts to ensure equality of opportunity and good race relations
- to raise public awareness of racial discrimination and injustice, and to win support for efforts to create a fairer and more equal society.

In addition, the CRE was charged with the responsibility of working towards a just and integrated society where diversity is valued and people are able to live free of all forms of racial discrimination.

The Macpherson Report into the death of Stephen Lawrence highlighted the fact that although direct discrimination was less common than in previous years, indirect discrimination was not only insidious but it was also more difficult to detect. In his report, Macpherson identified institutional racism as clouding the approach of the Metropolitan Police in investigating the death of Stephen Lawrence, a young black man.

The Race Relations (Amendment) Act 2000 builds on and extends the requirements of the 1976 Act. The 2000 Act gives public authorities a new statutory duty to promote race equality. The aim is to help public authorities to provide fair and accessible services, and to improve equal opportunities in employment.

DISABILITY

It is difficult to know the precise number of people with disability/ impairment in the country because, as well as those who are registered as disabled, there are countless others who, for a variety of reasons, are not registered. One area of agreement is that there is a large number of the population that is disabled. What constitutes disability is not always clear but the official definition of disability according to the Discrimination and Disability Act 1995: 2 is:

'There must be a mental or physical condition which has a substantial and long-term adverse affect on the employee's ability to carry out normal day-to-day activities. Long-term means that the condition must last, or be likely to last, for more than 12 months. The applicant's ability to carry out normal day-to-day activities can be adversely affected in one or more of the following ways:

- mobility
- manual dexterity
- physical co-ordination
- ability to lift or otherwise move everyday objects
- speech, hearing or eyesight
- memory or ability to concentrate, learn or understand
- understanding the risk of physical danger.'

The act helpfully spells out what was meant by physical and mental impairment:

- sensory impairments, including visual and hearing impairments
- learning disabilities/differences, including dyslexia
- mental illness
- severe disfigurements
- cancer
- HIV/AIDS
- progressive conditions even at an early stage
- conditions which are characterised by a number of cumulative effects such as pain or fatigue
- a past history of disability
- sensory impairments, including visual and hearing impairments.

Prior to the enactment of the DDA (1995), the Chronically Sick and Disabled Person Act 1970 was the main legislation that focused exclusively on the rights of disable people. Although now much derided for using what would now be considered abusive and unacceptable terms, the Act was quite innovative in many ways. For example, it required that all health and welfare authorities enquire into the numbers and needs of disabled people within their authority. The reasoning was twofold: to gather statistics for the authorities and organisations concerned but also to best organise their services. More radically perhaps, Section 21 of the Act required that public buildings be made accessible to people with a disability. Similarly, the places that were covered by the Public Health Act, such as inns, public houses, beer houses, refreshment houses or places of public entertainment, were also required to ensure that their facilities were accessible to everyone. In addition, the Act required that disabled people should have access and facilities at universities, schools, offices and other premises.

Clearly, the intention of the 1970 Act was to make it the responsibility of authorities and organisations to ensure that they engage with and provide appropriate provisions and services. The difficulty with the Act and subsequent acts that followed was that they lacked enforcement. The tone and language of the acts gave the impression that organisations may embark on ensuring access and providing services at their own convenience and if it was not too expensive. The Discrimination and Disability Act 1995 both entrenched the provisions already contained within the 1970 Act and extended it.

The DDA 1995 set out to protect disabled people from discrimination in areas such as education, property (management of buying, letting or renting) and land, employment, access to facilities, goods and services. The current batch of legislation, including DDA 1995, DDA 2005, on disability does appear to be more comprehensive and places greater responsibility on authorities and organisations, both private and public, to ensure that everyone has full access to services and provisions and that no one is disadvantaged because of their disability. The difficulty, in this and earlier legislation, is that there was a time lag between the implementation of the legislation and people, for whom it was intended, starting to feel the benefit. Although changing structures, systems and processes is crucial, it is equally important to change societal culture and general attitudes towards disability.

WHEN DIFFERENT DISCRIMINATIONS COLLIDE

It would be churlish to challenge the view that Britain is essentially a multi-cultural, multi-faith, tolerant, progressive and liberal democratic society. The challenge for anti-discriminatory practice in such a diverse society is how to reconcile opposing and, sometimes, incompatible ideas and beliefs. So, on the one hand, there is a call for anti-discriminatory practice to be universal in its recognition and treatment of discrimination, yet on the other hand there is often a call for a relativistic approach in the way it tackles different discriminatory practices. Britain, like some other countries in the European Union, sees itself as a safe haven and the birth place of democracy where individual freedoms are prized above all else. But what happens when some groups or individuals put forward arguments that they should be allowed exemptions from certain legislation and policies because of their cultural beliefs and religious doctrine, or these provisions clash against their values and beliefs?

For example, some religious groups believe it is within their scriptures to, effectively, discriminate against women or lesbians and gay men. There are some cultural groups who believe that women are not equal to men and they are not allowed to see or speak to any professionals from state agencies (such as social services, police, education, health workers) without the presence of a male member of the family or the woman's family in attendance. There are people who live in Britain and originate from countries (such as Jamaica, South Africa, Iran and many Middle Eastern countries) where it is not just that state agents persecute people because of their sexual orientation but gay men and lesbians also face violence, and in some cases even death from people in their neighbourhoods. In South Africa, lesbian women face unprecedented brutality as they live in constant fear of what has been termed 'corrective rape'. Corrective rape involves lesbian women being targeted and gang raped because of their sexual orientation by gangs of men.

Unlike some other countries, Britain has enacted many of the measures needed to protect the rights of people to live in relative peace without fear of discrimination. The tension appears to be between upholding these rights and listening to different points of view, particularly if they are being articulated by minorities who experience discrimination in society.

HUMAN RIGHTS LEGISLATION

The European Convention on Human Rights (ECHR) came into effect in Britain in 1998 and some would argue that it has transformed the relationship between the state and its subjects (citizens). Despite many of the criticisms levelled against it, the ECHR has enabled individuals and groups to challenge what they perceive as unfair and unjust treatment by state agents or others. In fact, there have been a number of landmark decisions that have upheld the principles that are entrenched in the Convention.[1] The ECHR was drafted after the Second World War and sets out 14 articles, which have since been added to by protocols to further reinforce existing rights and guaranteeing addition rights. Article 1 of the ECHR essentially sets the scene and proclaims that it is an 'Act to give greater effect to rights and freedoms guaranteed under the European Convention on Human Rights' (OPSi, 2008: 1). It is in Articles 2 to 14 that the various rights that everyone in society should enjoy are clearly set out.

None of the ECHR articles make any reference to sexual orientation although this is rectified by way of the Employment Equality (Sexual Orientation) (Amendment) Regulations 2003. The ECHR is seen by many as a quasi constitution that enhances the rights of individuals and protects them against persecution by the state and its agents and non-state groups and individuals. Perhaps it can be argued that the ECHR has superseded all other legislation with regard to discriminatory practices (although in practice the other anti-discriminatory legislations are still very much the first port of call for many people, including practitioners), because it specifically forbids all forms of persecution, discrimination and oppression.

SEXUAL ORIENTATION

Unlike other forms of discrimination, it is only relatively recently that sexual orientation has been accorded the same level of importance in legislation. Many of those who have been fighting to get sexual orientation recognised as of equal importance to other areas may well argue, and with some justification perhaps, that tackling homophobia has taken longer because of the prejudices that exist within oppressed groups. There is no single piece of legislation that makes it unlawful to discriminate against someone because of their sexual orientation and no single act to protect lesbian and gay people from abuse, harassment, victimisation, violence and discrimination. In essence, the legal protection of lesbian and gay people can be found in several Acts. For example, the Civil Partnership Act 2004 made it possible for lesbian and gay people

---

1   For a good historical overview of the ECHR, it is worth visiting the Liberty website – www.yourRights.org.uk

to get 'married' and to register as civil partners. The implication of this is that lesbian and gay couples in civil partnerships enjoy the same rights and legal status as married heterosexual couples. Similarly, the Employment Equality (Sexual Orientation) (Amendment) Regulations 2003 made it unlawful to deny a person a job because of prejudice about their sexual orientation. The Act gives individuals the right to take action if they have been denied an equal chance of training and promotion because of their sexual orientation. This is quite an important piece of legislation because it serves as the legal framework for protecting people who face discrimination because of their sexual orientation. The legislation is ultimately an amendment within employment law and appears not to cover the same ground as the other legislation that tackles other forms of discrimination. Although great strides have been made and there are promises of more changes to come, we would argue that currently many people still face discrimination and unfair treatment, often covertly, because of their sexual orientation.

RELIGIOUS BELIEF

This is a thorny area because historically Britain has been a broadly Christian country but has also become a multi-faith, parliamentary democracy. However, Richard Dawkins (2006: 380) observed that, 'In Britain, where we lack a constitutional separation between church and state, atheist parents usually go with the flow and let schools teach their children whatever religion prevails in the culture'. Even though Dawkins' observation is factually correct, people living in Britain would be hard pressed to provide evidence of religious indoctrination being mediated by the state. Although Dawkins is correct in his assertion that there is no constitution or legislation separating the church from the state, in reality a great deal of effort is made to separate religion from the state. For example, in state schools, children are involved in what is often described as a broadly Christian assembly. In fact, a broadly Christian assembly does not necessarily mean talking about Christianity but rather that the discussions are generally influenced by or based on humanistic philosophical ideas. In other words, non-religious state school assemblies are often about ethical consideration, encouraging children to think about other people, to be kind to others and to care about their environment, and to think about the impact of their attitudes and behaviour towards others, recognising and accepting difference and diversity and the nurturing of acceptance and tolerance. These may be ideals that are evident in the Christian faith but these sentiments are by no means confined to Christianity alone. It would not be a revelation to suggest that many other religions and religious groups also share these ideals. Interestingly, there is an increasing call to encourage Britain to be proud of its Christian roots rather than feeling embarrassed by it. There is a view that while Britain has encouraged multiculturalism, with its slogan of different but equal, there has been a neglect of the nurturing of a sense of national cohesion and a framework for a national identity. The charge against successive governments is that their approach has been to foster multiculturalism and encourage people to glorify in other people's cultures, ethnicity, identity and religious beliefs, while they have, unwittingly perhaps, discouraged national cohesion or any valorisation of all things that may be deemed British, whether it is its Christian background, national identity or its cultural values.

In Britain, there is no state persecution on religious grounds and people are generally left alone to practise their religion peacefully and untroubled by the state. Despite the non-interference, some religious groups do feel discriminated against and believe that they face greater obstacles in comparison to others in society. The blasphemy law in Britain goes back many centuries and its aim is essentially to protect the 'tenets and beliefs of the Church of England'. This clearly suggests that other Christian denominations and other religious groups cannot look to the blasphemy law for protection. Following a private prosecution for blasphemous libel in 1977, 'it was determined that a libel in this regard was committed if a publication about God, Christ, the Christian religion or the Bible used words which were scurrilous, abusive or offensive, which vilified Christianity and might lead to a breach of the peace' (Law Commission 1985: 130). There was an attempt by many Muslims, during the Salman Rushdie affair,[2] for the blasphemy law to be extended to include all religions. As the signatories of Article 19 (a group set up to support Rushdie and to challenge laws that attempt to protect all religions from criticisms) found, 'The Muslim community in Britain has thought to invoke the laws on blasphemy in their campaign to suppress *The Satanic Verses*. Distress over the novel can only have been increased with the discovery that the existing law protects Christianity alone and not other faiths such as Islam' (Article 19: 1). Despite the fierce debate that ensued, the blasphemy law was not

---

2   Salman Rushidie's book *The Satanic Verses* caused outrage in the Islamic world and the spiritual leader of Iran ordered that the author must be killed by issuing a fatwa.

extended nor was it repealed as had been hoped. Instead, under the EU Employment directive, Britain enacted the Employment Equality (Religion or Belief) Regulations 2003. This act effectively outlaws religious discrimination in employment and occupation. One of the main criticisms of the EU directive, and of the Act, is that unlike the Race Relations (Amendment) Act, it does not address the wider civil law areas because it does not extend discrimination (on religious or belief grounds), in the delivery of goods, facilities and services and there is no positive duty on organisations to promote religious tolerance and understanding. In many ways, despite its limitations, this is still an important piece of legislation because it recognises that discrimination on religious grounds involves lack of opportunity and exclusion from full participation in some areas in society.

COMMISSION FOR EQUALITY AND HUMAN RIGHTS

The Equal Opportunity Commission, the Disability Rights Commission and the Commission for Racial Equality were the three bodies charged with the duty and responsibilities to both police anti-discriminatory practices and to promote equality in society. Following the enactment and ratification of the European Convention on Human Rights (1998), it was deemed appropriate, and perhaps cost-effective, to bring the three bodies under a single structure. The birth of the Commission for Equality and Human Rights heralded an approach that could make a major difference to the way discrimination is both viewed and tackled. In our view, although the previous commissions were relatively effective in their different ways, they did not present a holistic view of discrimination. This led to a degree of fragmentation and lack of cohesion and there was some disconnection between the three bodies. This split rested on the notion that an individual has one single identity, when in reality a person's experience of discrimination may straddle different areas because of their complex and multiple identities. In this instance, a single body is not only all-encompassing, it also encourages a more integrative thinking and approach. The role of the Commission for Equality and Human Rights is to 'eliminate discrimination, reduce inequality, protect human rights and to build good relations, ensuring that everyone has a fair chance to participate in society' (CEHR 2008: 5). Furthermore, the body is charged with acting, 'not only for the disadvantaged, but for everyone in society, and can use its new enforcement powers where necessary to guarantee people's equality. It also has a mandate to promote understanding of the Human Rights Act' (CEHR 2008: 5). Unlike the previous commissions, the role of the CEHR is quite wide ranging and, as well as reactive elements, there are also expectations that it promotes equality, encourages good practice and fosters awareness and better understanding of human rights.

EQUAL OPPORTUNITY POLICIES

At the local and practice level, equal opportunities policies draw on all the legislation described in this chapter. Having drawn on a number of legislative frameworks, the driving force has been to develop and define sets of principles and values that are characteristic of anti-discriminatory practice. Organisations and institutions set out their policies as statements of intent that show a commitment that they value diversity and difference; that they believe in justice and fairness and would not perpetuate or reinforce any form of discrimination. This commitment applies both to people having access to services and a promise to challenge discriminatory attitudes and practices within the organisation. In an effort to make their intensions clear, the commitment is translated into practice guidelines for staff. It often sets out expectations and requirements and it is envisaged that both their staff and the service users who use their services or rely on their provisions adhere to the policies. Much emphasis is placed on how all staff members of the organisation should interact with service users and the appropriate manner in which they should conduct the businesses of the organisation.

In order to fulfil their commitments, many organisations and institutions go through a process in developing their equal opportunities policies. The approach taken may either involve the whole organisation or a small group of people within the organisation. It is not unusual for an organisation effectively to employ an external consultant to help them develop a policy. Whichever approach is adopted, the aim (with input from all other members) is to develop a policy and a statement that captures both the ethos and character of anti-discriminatory practice. Although each organisation and institution tailors its statement and policy to suit the context in which they operate, they tend to use the same format and the statements have similar content. So, for example, the policy itself would contain a preamble, which is essentially the rationale, followed by aims and objectives (what it aims to provide, challenge, ensure, promote, etc.), and finally the implementation procedure. The good policies tend to have preventative as well as supportive measures and they include procedures for monitoring and evaluating the policy and dealing with complaints that may arise.

There is no single equal opportunity legislation (though promoting equal opportunities is mentioned in the Race Relations (Amendment) Act 2000), rather *equal opportunity policies* are extrapolations of ideas from many, if not all, of the primary legislations that have been enacted to tackle all forms of discrimination in society. Organisations and institutions' equal opportunity policies and the accompanying statements have served to act as the frontline for guarding against prejudices and discriminatory practices. In many ways, they have proven quite effective in raising general awareness of the nature and pervasiveness of discriminations in the workplace and in society in general.

CONCLUSION

The aim of this chapter has been to set out the range of legislation that attempts to challenge discrimination and discriminatory practices in society. We believe, despite their individual failings, that all the legislation has made a significant difference in practitioners' practice. They have also impacted on society's attitude towards those who experience discrimination. In comparison to many other countries, it would be inconceivable that private organisations, statutory institutions or publicly funded organisations in the UK would, as a matter of policy, set out deliberately to discriminate against people because of their background, gender or disability. Generally speaking, discriminatory attitudes and behaviour are deemed unacceptable by a large section of the population and there is a great deal of effort made by individuals, institutions and organisations to challenge them wherever possible. Although it is difficult to ascertain a precise figure to support the assertion that society is more accepting and tolerant of diversity, the mere fact that many organisations and institutions see diversity as an important area to consider and that an anti-discriminatory practice approach is worthy enough to pursue and implement, reinforces our view that there has indeed been a change in attitudes towards discrimination. There are now policies, systems and processes that have been put in place by many organisations and institutions in an effort to combat discriminatory practices. We would argue that, despite their shortcomings, a cursory glance at existing legislation would reveal that, far from being reactive or mere tokenistic gestures, the current batch of legislation has attempted to be supportive and facilitative and is based on promoting fairness and equality in society. Each of the different legislation has attempted to provide a safeguard against discrimination and unfair treatment, but the question has yet to be answered as to the extent to which the European Convention on Human Rights supersedes and provides a better support and safeguard for everyone in society.

Points to ponder

It is asserted by some that the ECHR is a charter for unfairness and illogical interpretation. It is suggested that a British Bill of Rights would be more appropriate in addressing the relationship between the state and its citizens.

- What is wrong with ECHR?
- Why would a British Bill of Rights be necessary and how would it differ from ECHR?
- What is the main role and function of the Commission for Equality and Human Rights?

The DDA (1995) defines disability as: 'There must be a mental or physical condition which has a substantial and long-term adverse affect on the employee's ability to carry out normal day-to-day activities'.

- What is the problem with this definition?

Part Two
Implementation and
Practice Considerations

6
Working with Diversity and Challenging the Status Quo

diversity and challenge

INTRODUCTION

It is generally regarded as a truism that where you stand affects your point of view; this follows the Kantian notion that we (human beings) see things not as they are but as we are. Many individuals and organisations would acknowledge that there have been major improvements in many of the areas that were previously of concern in the 1960s, 1970s, 1980s and 1990s. However, it would also be accepted that although there have been improvements, discrimination has not completely disappeared from society. For example, many welfare agencies and organisations have worked very hard to address the problem of discrimination in their service provision and increase the diversity of their workforce. It is evident that interviewing processes, training courses, disciplinary procedures and general policies have been put in place to ensure that both practitioners and service users are aware of the agency/organisation's anti-discriminatory stance. Similarly, many individuals have made great efforts to address their preconceptions and their negative views about 'others'. They have been persuaded by the argument that there are people who face discrimination, injustice and unfairness because of their sexual orientation, race, gender, disability, religious belief, social class and age. Even though discriminatory attitudes still prevail in many instances, it is unlikely that the crude and derogatory utterances and behaviours that were so prevalent and were once deemed acceptable would now go unchallenged. Also, great strides have been made in ensuring that those who hold such views would, at least, be made to feel uncomfortable. As cautioned by Preston-Shoot (2008), this is not to suggest discrimination no longer exists or people no longer hold negative views, but the point we are making is that there has been a noticeable change in society's outlook and discriminatory practices are certainly not as overt or blatant as in the past.

Others may argue that in fact discrimination and discriminatory practices are still as prevalent as they were before and that each new generation of professional needs to relearn the lessons of the past and bring new insights to bear on the field of ADP, and diversity.

THE CHANGING LANDSCAPE

It is evident from any reading of their policies and procedures that many organisations, agencies and institutions, including government departments, have been addressing the problem of discrimination and, at the same time, individuals in society have accepted the need to tackle discrimination in all its forms. However, there are renewed tensions about discrimination in society in general. The catalyst for this renewed tension comes from two sources which have served to change the social landscape of the UK. Firstly, over the last few years, as a result of the expansion of membership of the European Union, there has been an increase in the number of settlers from Eastern Europe, and, secondly, there has been a relatively high number of people seeking asylum and those obtaining refugee status. As new migrant groups have joined the country, old battles that had been fought for and gains made (for example, in the areas of race, class, gender and sexuality) have had to be revisited. There is anecdotal evidence that some of the new arrivals come from societies where any aspects of discrimination have barely been raised let alone tackled. Some of these groups and individuals have brought with them negative views and stereotypical ideas about other people that were once in evidence in Britain in earlier decades. In some cases, some of the new entrants were unused to living in a liberal, multi-racial and multicultural society. So although the focus has been to deepen the gains that have already been made in tackling discrimination, it would appear that there is a need also to ensure that the new groups and individuals coming into the country are 'assimilated' into the notions of fairness, justice and non-discriminatory attitudes and behaviour.

However, it is fair to say that the newcomers from Eastern Europe and those that are refugees or asylum seekers from non-European countries, face particular difficulties of their own because they are seen as the ones who are competitors for and beneficiaries of scarce resources. What is emerging in this new landscape is a clash between the newcomers and the denizens, who now also include those who had previously experienced discrimination when they were the newcomers. The fault lines are not necessarily confined to the usual areas of race, class, gender, sexual orientation, impairment or age, but it is something more nebulous. The concerns straddle a number of different areas and include both the metaphorical and geographical 'spaces' that are occupied by the new arrivals. They also include economic considerations, their entitlement to state provision and their 'foreignness'. This is quite an interesting new take on an old topic. Of course, many of the earlier migrants were from Commonwealth countries and were therefore linked to the United Kingdom through the colonial experience. Thus, they possessed a shared colonial legacy, a shared language and social ties to Britain, having come from countries that saw Britain as the mother country. The new arrivals, typically Somalis, Kurds, Eastern Europeans, South Americans and people from the Middle East, have a very different historic relationship with the United Kingdom. Although there was a colonial presence in some of the Middle Eastern countries, the link forged between the United Kingdom and those countries was very different in comparison to those that was forged with the Commonwealth countries.

BEYOND A BINARY WORLD VIEW

As we have tried to demonstrate throughout this book, anti-discriminatory practice is a far more complex concept than is usually imagined or articulated. The approach that has frequently been taken in discussing and exploring anti-discriminatory practice has often been simplistic and, in many cases, ill thought out. In many publications that encourage anti-discriminatory practice, a binary world view is presented in which one is either white or black, male or female, old or young, heterosexual or homosexual, disabled or non-disabled.

The creation of a binary world was a simple and uncomplicated way of making sense of a society that appeared to be changing, confusing and fluid. In our view, this approach to anti-discriminatory practice was fuelled and underpinned by a quasi-separatist philosophical perspective. In this perspective, the world is neatly divided into two opposing camps. On the one side of the divide are those that have been identified as oppressed (be they service users, minority groups, women, the working class, people with impairment, lesbian and gay people), and on the other side are the oppressors (men, white people, heterosexuals, the non-disabled and the middle class). The oppressors are viewed as the beneficiaries of all that the state has to offer; they have better employment and employment prospects, easy access to services and provisions, are well served by the health and education system and are not over-represented in the mental health or penal system. Their class or group control all areas of society and they reinforce and perpetuate their position by excluding others.

In this world view, all service users are depicted as victims, in some capacity, who are locked in a cycle of dependence by the very system that was created to help and support them. There is the feeling that service users are at the mercy of social services and social workers and that they have little active involvement in planning and organising the help and support that are provided to them. In this perspective social workers are little more than agents of the state who are intent on making service users' lives a misery and coercing them into toeing the state's line. There is an unchallengeable assumption that practitioners do not really care about services users nor are they concerned about making a difference in people's lives (Okitikpi and Aymer 2008).

More recently, social work has had a renewed focus on and impetus about service-user involvement and participation in their care and in service delivery. Social work education has focused most strongly on service-user involvement in the planning of courses, the selection and assessment of students and the delivery of the curriculum. However, it seems to us that social work has set up a new binary: the professional/ service user nexus which has served only to reverse the old binary. Whenever binaries are set up, the end result is to invest 'goodness' in one group and 'badness' in the other.

Practitioners are thus thought to be out of touch with the realities of service users' lives and they are deemed either to possess no expertise or to use their expertise only to oppress service users. Rather, practitioners are expected to respond, without question, to the demands of service users since they are the experts of their own problems, and therefore know best. Practitioners are embarrassed to describe themselves as experts of human problems and that they are capable of making a difference in people's lives through an approach that relies on more than mere common sense. This could be described as perhaps an unfair caricature of how people generally view practitioners in relation to service users. But it is worth considering how the current discussions about user involvement are framed and the place and role afforded to practitioners. In our view, taking such a simplistic and binary approach is unhelpful. We need new ways of thinking about ADP.

The binary approach is not only essentialist in nature, but it also relies on cultural absolutism, biological determinism and moral relativism. For example, it is usual for literature on anti-discriminatory practice (be it on race, gender, sexual orientation or impairment/disability) to tend to assume a great deal and as a result target the 'Other' rather than approaching it from a more universal perspective. So, in the past, work on anti-racist practice had a target audience of primarily white practitioners in mind with no consideration given to the reality of non-white practitioners and that they too could be oppressive or discriminatory both in their attitudes and in their approach. Also, work on looking at disability/impairment tended to assume that there are people with disability and then there is the rest of the population. Similarly, discussion about sexism ran into difficulty by seeing all women as a mass without recognising the difference between women, and moreover all men were castigated as sexist by nature.

The challenge is to be able to theorise more than one difference at a time. This suggests a much more difficult and complicated politics, because the sides are not given in advance, nor in neat divisions.

NOT BLAMING THE VICTIM

It is understandable why the binary approach was preferred during the 1970s and 1980s, because in that period there were no other alternatives and the issues seemed relatively clear-cut. At that time, black people, women, people with impairments, lesbians and gay people faced overt discrimination and oppression not just from individuals but also from the state. The struggle during the period was not only about fairness and justice but also for society as a whole to recognise that there was abuse, violence and systematic oppression of many sections of the population. Understanding the background to anti-discriminatory practice is important because it locates the present in a wider context and allows for a more informed analysis. Asking for a more honest and broader reconsideration of discrimination is not intended as a way of placating 'oppressors' and blaming the 'victims'. On the contrary, the desire is to expose what is widely known and already openly discussed among academics, practitioners and others involved in the world of health and social care. One of the difficulties about implementing anti-discriminatory practice in its current form is that it is too narrow in its scope because it focuses on the group that is deemed to be the oppressor and placates and assuages those who see themselves as the oppressed (or victims). The result is that many people don't necessarily think that anti-discriminatory practice applies to them because they are the oppressed.

We state strongly that, as a starting point, no one group or individual has a monopoly on being oppressed or being the oppressor. We wish to move from the either/or world view to a both/and world view. In other words, everyone and every group has the capability of being both an oppressor and being oppressed by others. In essence, people are able to be both victim and perpetrator at the same time.

THE POWER DIMENSION

One of the reasons given for not acknowledging the fact that discrimination (racism, homophobia, sexism, ageism and disablism) is not restricted to particular individuals or groups is that those who are oppressed lack power in society. In other words, people who are oppressed may be discriminatory in their attitudes but they lack the necessary power to put their negative attitudes and behaviour into effect. This definition of power and how it is exercised is flawed. It is based on a vertical structure where those at the top have power over those deemed to be at the bottom. This analysis owes more to 18th and early 19th century thinking and it is based on a rigid analysis of society and the social structure. Of course, there are power bases in the United Kingdom, for example the monarchy, the political class, the fourth estate (the press and media), and many of the organs of the state. But these are power structures and therefore irrespective of the individuals that occupy the structure, power would still be able to be exercised. In our view, within the United

Kingdom's context, the distribution of power is more akin to Foucault's analysis. In other words, power is far more diffused and complicated because it is as much about social interaction as it is about power structures. Sarup (1993) highlighted that Foucault (1976) observed that the power relations between people shape their social interaction, and to exercise power is both to impose particular practices and relationships and to define another's reality. Trying to apply how others define social interactions and people's realities may prove difficult. Although Foucault's (1976) observation is interesting as it highlights how power may be exercised, this analysis owes more to a totalitarian and coercive society than a matured liberal democratic one. Foucault's analysis reinforced the general approach described earlier in which the oppressor exercises power over the oppressed. This approach reduces people to the role of puppets, without any free will and incapable of exercising judgement or control over their lives. This is a very pessimistic, deterministic and unyielding understanding of power relations between people in this society.

KEY CONCEPTS

SEXISM

Discriminatory attitudes and behaviours towards women start from early childhood through to adulthood. In many instances in the education system, there are lower expectations on young girls despite the fact they outperform boys at all academic levels at secondary school. In some cases, it is not the educational system that is at fault but parents and guardians who have very low or no aspirations for girl children in the family. Acknowledging that sexism is not only confined to men's attitude and their behaviour is, again, not to suggest that women are responsible for sexism or suggest that men are not culpable in the perpetuation of sexism. Rather, it is to make known publicly what is accepted privately that society as a whole is guilty of reinforcing many of the public and private inequalities that women experience in society. Despite the enactment of all the different anti-discriminatory legislation, women continue to struggle to enjoy the same level of income and command the same level of opportunity as men, particularly in some occupations. The negative and discriminatory attitude towards women is also evident in the criminal justice system, particularly in the poor level of conviction in cases involving violence towards women and in rape cases. Temkin and Krahe (2008) found in their study high-level misrepresentation and stereotypical assumptions about women who have been raped. In addition, there are also fewer numbers of women Queen's Counsels (QCs) and judges in comparison to their male counterparts.

There is ample evidence to support the assertion that women are still underrepresented in many occupational areas in society and as a result they fair less well economically in comparison to men. For example, a report on the research carried out by the Trade Union Congress found that women in their 30s earn 11.2 per cent less than their male counterparts. The figure increases to 22.8 per cent for women in their 40s. Carvel reported that 'the long hours and intensity of senior positions deterred mothers from seeking promotions for which they are qualified. Pay and grading systems were commonly based on a male skill set that undervalued so-called soft skills, and women tended to cluster in lower-paid jobs' (2008: 7). Banyard (2008) reinforced Carvel's analysis by highlighting the point that, 'The paucity of senior flexible roles, and the long working hours culture, shuts women out of the boardroom and forces them into lower paid, lower-status jobs when they have children' (Banyard 2008, quoted in Carvel 2008: 7).

DISABILITY

People with disability (impairment) have struggled for many years to have the same level of recognition, about their experiences of discrimination, as women and minority groups. As well as discrimination at the day-to-day level (in terms of attitudes), they also face inequalities in the lack of access to general spaces as enjoyed by the rest of the population, poor level of education, inadequate health provisions and lack of meaningful occupational opportunities. In many respects, prior to the enactment of the Disability Discrimination Act 2005, the Chronically Sick and Disabled Person Act 1970 was a landmark piece of legislation because it encouraged local authorities and organisations to consider and try to meet the needs of people with disability. The difficulty with this legislation and many of the others that followed was that the provisions contained within it were read as optional and were therefore ignored. People with disability (impairment) have had to battle the underlying assumption that because they have a disability, they are somehow 'different' to the rest of the population. They are treated as if they do not have the same wants, aspirations, hopes and rights. At best, they are on the extreme margins of society and at worst they are treated as non-existent objects to be pitied and kept out of view of the non-disabled. For many, all the social spaces and structures of society are essentially geared for non-disabled people and the near exclusion of people with disability from these social spaces and structures all contribute towards reinforcing a binary world view. The general attitudes towards people with disability continue to be influenced by a distorted and ill-informed understanding of the nature and range of disabilities. The situation is further compounded by what can only be described as apprehension and fear of disability. Yet, while there are people born with disability, many more people become disabled for a host of reasons. Disability is of course not confined to any particular group and indeed it transcends class, race, gender, sexual orientation, ethnicity or religious affiliations.

RACISM

Racism, like sexism and class (for a time at least) has been one of the dominant features of anti-discriminatory practice. In general, race was used as a demarcation line between white and black people. Essentially, black meant people born in the Caribbean Islands and people from Africa and their descendants. Also included among this group were those born of mixed parentage – these are people that have one black and one white parent. The premise for classifying them as black is based on the one-drop rule, a doctrine that posits that a drop of black blood automatically renders the person black (Okitikpi 2005). For a period, Southern Asian people (Indians, Pakistanis and Bangladeshis) were not really included in the black category, but this changed in the 1980s. Prior to the use of the term black to embrace all, people from Southern Asia faced the same kinds of discrimination as Africans and Caribbean people but rather than being referred to as black they were labelled 'Pakis'. As already discussed earlier, those identified as black or Asian faced overt and covert discrimination in many different areas because of the colour of their skins. Interestingly, for a brief period in the 1980s, the term black was given a radical political edge. It became fashionable for those who experienced discrimination, because of their cultural background or ethnicity, to seek refuge under the 'black' banner. So, for example, many Irish people, because of their experience of racism, started referring to themselves as black and attending black empowerment groups. The categorisation of people into races has its roots in scientific racism (Fryer 1984), and the belief that white people are the superior race and black people are essentially savages that need to be tamed and made more civilised. Even though this notion is now discredited (Rex 1970; Banton 1984; Fryer 1984; Jahoda 1999), its residue continues to form the basis of the relationship between black and white people. However, in our view, despite the social currency that the terms black and white still command, there is a need to now take account of the changing nature of society. Dividing people in society as being either black or white is increasingly difficult to maintain. There are now so many different groups of people in society who originate from all around the world that such simplistic classification can no longer be sustained. For example, although Egyptians, Moroccans and Tunisians are from Africa their colouration and ethnicity is quite different from Southern, Eastern and West Africans. Similarly, Middle Eastern Arabs are different from Jews even though they are from the same region. In addition, New-Zealander Maoris are not black but neither are they white. In fact, although their features are different from a North African, their colouration is quite similar. People forming relationships outside their cultural groups have made such classification even more complex. In essence, the point being made is that it is no longer sustainable to use race as a euphemism for referring to people in society. Also, the level of mixture as a result of interracial relationships and the increase in the numbers of Arabs and people from the Mediterranean, Middle-East and Sub-Sahara Africa further makes the old black and white demarcation unsustainable.

CLASS

Class was, for many years, the main focus of all those interested in challenging discrimination in all its forms. In fact for a period in the early 1960s and late 1970s, (Sivanandan 1990), all other areas (for example, race, gender, disability, sexual orientation) were considered to be of secondary consideration in comparison to the pivotal role of one's class in society. There was a genuine belief that once class was tackled, it would act as a catalyst to eradicating all other areas of inequalities. Class was perceived as the main dividing line between people in society. It was argued that irrespective of gender, race, sexual orientation or religious beliefs, it was one's class position that was the deciding factor in the level of discrimination that one experiences. However, at the same time as class was being championed, there was some disquiet amongst certain groups who believed that white males had hijacked the class struggle. The fissure that ensued resulted in the marginalisation of class as a means of understanding the nature of the social relations in society.

In place of class as an overarching explanation for social inequalities, a more fragmented approach was adopted. This effectively pitted sexual politics, queer identity, race and culture against each other. This fragmentation of groups into their own 'personal identity space' effectively left little room for class. What has now happened is that while much is discussed about many areas of discrimination, there is very little consideration given to the experiences of the white working class, particularly boys. It is evident that in many publications reference to poverty is really a euphemism for class; however, in our view, while some working-class people are in poverty, not all of them are. In addition, while the focus has been on race, religion, and disability and gender, the group that has been most neglected are *white working-class young men*. It is almost taboo to highlight the reality that white working-class boys face the same kinds of difficulties and problems as African-Caribbean boys, including the fact that their gender and colour does affect their life chances. Rather than consider white working-class boys as experiencing discrimination as other groups, they are often vilified and perceived to be the main perpetrators of discrimination in society. They are afforded very little opportunity to vent their anger and frustration against what they experience as injustice and unfairness in the way they have been excluded and treated by 'everyone' in their own country.

INVISIBLE GROUPS

Over the past 20 years, there have been concerted efforts to ensure that all forms of discrimination are not only highlighted but great efforts are made to challenge them wherever they occur and, in addition, when possible legislation is enacted to eradicate them. The kinds of crude discriminatory attitudes and practices that were endemic throughout the 1970s and earlier part of the 1980s are no longer tolerated generally in society. There is no doubt that much has been achieved in attempting to combat all forms of discrimination. However, the interesting point now though is that while there is still a great deal to be done to entrench the gains, there are certain groups that face not only discrimination in society at large but also difficulties from within their own cultural groups. It is ironic that those who have direct experience of the physical, emotional and psychological damage that discrimination can cause should themselves perpetuate discriminatory practices against others. While race, gender, sexual orientation and disability have enjoyed a high profile, buried within all the cacophony of discrimination, oppression and inequalities are the experiences of invisible groups whose voices are often drowned out. For example, it is no secret that lesbians and gay men (in particular) face discrimination and intolerance within the black community and some religious communities. There is little evidence of general acceptances within the African and, in particular, the African-Caribbean community and some religious groups of lesbians and gays. The intolerance towards this group is so entrenched that it is difficult to have any rational discussion on the matter. There is incredulity among many people in the African and the African-Caribbean community that their negative views and homophobic attitudes should even be challenged. There is what could best be described as folklore by some members of these communities, the belief that homosexuality is essentially a white European notion that has been exported to Africa and the Caribbean. As a result, the experiences of *black lesbians and gay* people are akin to the experiences of white lesbians and gays in the 1970s. At best, they face ostracism from their family and their community; at worst, they face abuse, humiliation and physical violence because of their sexual orientation. It is worth making the point that the reasons for highlighting the homophobic views and attitudes that exist within the African and Caribbean communities is not to demonise the people in these communities or suggest that they are more homophobic compared to other communities in the UK. Rather, it is to acknowledge what is, in essence, an open secret but that people are afraid, for whatever reason, to express. In our view, anti-discriminatory practice requires honesty, openness and the ability to challenge discrimination in all its different forms wherever it may exist.

RELIGIOUS TOLERANCE

Religious tolerance is one of the most important pillars of Britain's liberal democracy. Although there is no formal separation of the state from religion, there is however a general unspoken acceptance that religion is a private matter and should therefore not play such a dominant role in society. As a result, people are left to practise their religious belief, whatever it is and however outlandish, so long as they are broadly within the law. However, despite the high level of tolerance, there are concerns about the increasing tensions between different religious groups in society. For example, *Muslims, Jews, Hindus* and *Sikhs* have all experienced varying degrees of discrimination and violence because of their beliefs. However, while those interested in challenging discriminatory practices have been very good at identifying both the nature and, in many cases, the sources of the violence and hate campaign against these religious groups, very little is said about the intolerance of some religious groups. The other groups that are often not given such a high profile are *older people* from minority backgrounds and *travellers*. These two groups are often isolated and, in the case of travellers, have to battle local authorities for basic services that by law they are entitled to.

MAKING SENSE OF THE NEW REALITIES

Anti-discriminatory practice should not discriminate between groups or individuals in society. Its main goal has always been to challenge discriminatory practices and encourage an approach that is person-centred within a framework of humanitarian consideration. If anti-discriminatory practice works on the assumption that there is a clear demarcation between those who are oppressed and those who are oppressors then, in our view, it is bound to fall into difficulties. Such simplistic demarcation ignores the complex nature of human interactions and the fact that people embody a myriad of forms. To divide people into such neat categories of either being oppressed or an oppressor is both deterministic and, interestingly, discriminatory. It is also difficult to maintain the assumption that those who experience discrimination and oppression are incapable of having attitudes or behaving in a way that is both discriminatory and oppressive. Anti-discriminatory practice has to have the confidence of challenging discriminations irrespective of the origin or background of the perpetrators. It has to recognise that challenging people with deep religious convictions about their hatred of or negative views of homosexuality does not automatically equate to religious intolerance, but a questioning of the basic foundation upon which such views are held. It is also to challenge the compatibility of such views with the values, expectations and ethos embedded within anti-discriminatory practice. Similarly, challenging individuals and groups about their childrearing practices, attitudes towards women, family life, social outlook and world view are not, in our view, tantamount to cultural imperialism or Eurocentric thinking. Rather, it is implicit in anti-discriminatory practice that some behaviour, attitudes, values and beliefs are not acceptable and are, therefore, incompatible with anti-discriminatory practice. Unlike other ideas (positive discrimination, affirmative action and quota systems), anti-discriminatory practice is not about valorising some groups or individuals above others or about championing the cause of some groups and individuals instead of others.

CONCLUSION

Despite the major changes that have occurred in society and the progressive attitudes and tolerance that are fostered, discrimination continues to be of concern. Discriminatory practices are not just confined to institutions and organisations but individuals, groups and communities too are culpable in perpetuating attitudes and views that are incompatible with anti-discriminatory values. Those who discriminate do so for a number of reasons and while some may be able to articulate both their reasons and motivation for discriminating against people they neither know nor understand, others may find it more difficult to express themselves and provide a rationale for their beliefs, attitudes and behaviour. It is our contention that it is simply not the case that people who experience oppression are not able to discriminate or oppress others because they lack political power in society. Anti-discriminatory practice is a transformative concept in that it believes that people are capable of making a difference, for the better, in the lives of others. The aim of this chapter has been to suggest that in order for anti-discriminatory practice to remain relevant, it needs to move beyond a binary world view.

Points to ponder

Consider the situations outlined below and think about how you would respond to them. Would your response be dependent on the colour, gender or race of the practitioner?

1. A social work practitioner who is a British-born Muslim who says openly that he/she hates Western values and mores.
2. A social work lecturer practitioner who is proud to proclaim that their approach is Afrocentric. What is the significance of their utterance within the context of anti-discriminatory practice?
3. A woman social work practitioner who calls for men to be excluded from working with children because all men are deemed to be 'potential' perpetrators of child sexual abuse.
4. White working-class boys do not have the same problems as others and they are more likely to be perpetrators of racial discrimination.

7

Key Skills, Knowledge and Anti-discriminatory Practice

Introduction
Rethinking anti-discriminatory practice
A proactive approach
Engaging with anti-discriminatory practice
Key concepts
Language use
The power of communication
Assessment
Introspective, reflexive and reflective practice
Conclusion

INTRODUCTION

One of the themes that we hope has remained constant throughout this book is the acknowledgement that anti-discriminatory practice is not as easy as it is often portrayed. This is not to suggest that the approach is too difficult or impracticable in the face of other pressures. Indeed, far from it, our experience of working with lecturers, students and practitioners in varying practices and education settings attests to the fact that people who are committed to the concept are readily able to incorporate it into their approach, despite the obstacles they may experience. Anti-discriminatory practice is about human rights, fairness, social and economic equality, and justice for all. Spelt out in this form, it seems difficult to comprehend why anyone would think that it is acceptable to be discriminatory, not just in the practice setting but also in all other aspects of life. At its core, anti-discriminatory practice:

fosters an approach that challenges preconceptions about a (racially, cultural, gender, sexuality, ethnically, disability, age, class) binary world. It is an approach that understands the wider societal discourse of injustices and discrimination and the power imbalance in society. (Okitikpi 2004: 131)

On close examination of the obstacles to anti-discriminatory practice, it soon becomes clear that the objections owe a great deal to the kind of attitudes and thinking that was characteristic of the pre-enlightenment era. Then as now, views, knowledge and understanding of different people in society were informed by superstitions, belief in the superiority of certain groups in society to rule over others, and religious authorities that believed they had the right to control people's personal and social affairs. As we have already acknowledged in earlier chapters, society has changed profoundly as has the nature of the social relationships between people in society. However, although there have been major social changes, in some areas, things have altered unrecognisably; some of the current attitudes would not be too unfamiliar to the people that lived in the pre-enlightenment era. Sometimes when listening to discussion about race, class, sexual orientation, gender and disability, it is difficult to believe that the age of enlightenment actually happened. Or that there is recognition that despite the constraints that exist in people's lives there is such a thing as free will and people are capable of making choices. In its current guise, ill-informed views about others, over-zealous religious beliefs and superstitious beliefs about sexual orientation and disability have given way to a strident attitude about the rights and freedom of individuals and groups to maintain their (often negative) views and bigoted attitudes towards others. The mantra of a liberal and multicultural society is that people should have the right to maintain their racial identity, their religious beliefs, culture values and ethnic identity and personal beliefs. It champions the view that no one has a right to impose their values on others and that there are no rights and wrongs. There is an assertion that everyone has a right to be heard and their views and perspectives should be accommodated in society.

While on the surface it would seem like a good idea to adhere to these sentiments, in reality what it has encouraged, in some at least, is intolerance, racism, sexism, homophobia and a separatist and essentialist perspective. In our view, euphemistic nuances such as respecting 'difference', separate but equal, maintaining cultural authenticity and respecting religious beliefs, encourage and reinforce dogmatism and support and perpetuate the notion of the 'other'. This, we are certain, is not what was intended when ideas about anti-discriminatory practice were being developed. Instead of questioning and challenging discrimination, it has had the effect of perpetuating and entrenching discriminatory views and attitudes in some people. Attempting anti-discriminatory practice under such circumstances is not only confusing, it is also practically impossible.

RETHINKING ANTI-DISCRIMINATORY PRACTICE

One of the key reasons why many practitioners find it difficult to incorporate anti-discriminatory practice into their work is because of the way it is currently interpreted. Anti-discriminatory practice is sometimes treated as if it is only about developing awareness and being non-judgemental rather than also about acquiring certain sets of skills. This is why practitioners and students, when asked about how their practice is anti-discriminatory, often respond by saying that they are non-judgemental, that they act as *enablers, work in partnership* and *empower* service users. They may also mention that they use non-discriminatory language and that they are conscious of the impact and effects of the power difference between themselves and the service user. Some may also make reference to the importance of body posture and being aware of non-verbal signals. Furthermore, some may say that they are guided and influenced by all the areas identified by Langan and Day (1992).

Briefly, Langan and Day observed that:

> The attempt to construct an anti-discriminatory social work has taken shape out of a growing recognition of the specificities of oppression, according to gender, race, class, age, disability and sexual orientation. It emphasizes the diversity of experience and the validity of each person's experiences. It seeks to develop an understanding of both the totality of oppression and its specific manifestations as the preconditions for developing an anti-discriminatory practice relevant to all spheres of social work. (1992: 3)

It is evident that students and practitioners are able to freely discuss and provide a cogent description of anti-discriminatory practice as a philosophical concept, but often what is more difficult (and many do struggle to give a clear description) is to provide practical examples of how they have been able to implement the concept in their day-to-day practice.

A PROACTIVE APPROACH

It is worth revisiting Langan's point, which was well made, because it does provide a very good foundation for anti-discriminatory practice. Adams et al. (2002), Horner (2003) and Thompson (2006), in their different ways, also make similar observations. This assertion, about the underpinning foundation for anti-discriminatory practice, unsurprisingly perhaps, complements the ethos and the philosophical underpinning of the social work profession. As the International Federation of Social Workers rightly reported:

> Social work has grown out of humanitarian and democratic ideals. Its values base is about respect for the dignity and equality and worth of all people. The main aim of social work is to alleviate poverty, liberate vulnerable and oppressed people with the ultimate aim to promote social inclusion. (2003: 5)

In essence, both the International Federation of Social Workers, in their definition of the nature and ideals of social work, and Langan, in her view about the construction of anti-discriminatory practice, recognise the wide and inclusive nature of social work practice. Rather than settling for a definition of anti-discriminatory practice that is narrow and single issue dominated, there is an acknowledgement and an acceptance that it is a concept that has a much wider remit. It transcends individualised personal identity politics (though this is clearly important and forms part of its concerns) and takes account of the totality of people's experiences. It also takes account of people's social realities as well as the role of the socio-structural environment in which they live. In our view, anti-discriminatory practice was wrongly assumed to be a passive approach that did not address the political or the socio-structural dimension. It is thought that the concept was not concerned about problems of social inequalities, social class differentiation, domestic violence and the various other social problems and inequalities that exist in society. As already mentioned, in order to address what was perceived as the deficiencies of ADP, anti-oppressive practice was developed to inject a more radical political edge to practice. Dominelli (1993) defined anti-oppressive practice as:

> a form of social work practice which addresses social divisions and structural inequalities in the work that is done with clients (users) or workers. Anti-oppressive practice aims to provide more appropriate and sensitive

services by responding to people's needs regardless of their social status. Anti-oppressive practice embodies a person-centred philosophy, an egalitarian value system concerned with reducing the deleterious effects of structural inequalities upon people's lives; a methodology of focusing on both process and outcome; a way of structuring relationships between individuals and aims to empower users by reducing negative effects of hierarchy in their immediate interaction and the work they do together. (1993: 24)

It seems to us this definition actually encapsulates much of the ethos and philosophical underpinning of anti-discriminatory practice. It still seems unclear why there was a need to develop a different concept to tackle the problem of discrimination and inequalities when one already existed. Interestingly, anti-oppressive practice takes quite a narrow approach because it focuses primarily on external factors. In comparison, we believe anti-discriminatory practice takes a holistic approach because, as already mentioned, it is interested in both the external and internal aspects of people's experiences. More specifically, it is our contention that anti-discriminatory practice does not only focus on structures, systems, processes, organisations and external factors, it also recognises the role that people's attitudes and beliefs have on discriminatory practices. More crucially, anti-discriminatory practice understands the complexities inherent in human relationships and interactions.

ENGAGING WITH ANTI-DISCRIMINATORY PRACTICE

Working in a way that fully engages with the ethos and guiding principles of anti-discriminatory practice requires a great deal from the practitioner. For example, to be workable, it is essential that the practitioner take a constructive approach (rather than an oppositional outlook) in their view of the world and in the way they interact with people, organisations, systems and processes. They would also need to appreciate that the political dimension that informs anti-discriminatory practice is forged from the ideals of progressive liberation movements and it is rooted in a belief in social justice, egalitarianism, humanitarianism and the values and rights entrenched in the European Convention on Human Rights. The need to take account of these wider considerations is crucial to developing both a better understanding of the concept and in order to fully integrate it into daily practice. This, in essence, is the point that Brofrenbrenner (1979) articulates in developing the ecological system with respect to human development and made by Thompson (2003a), in his Personal, Social and Cultural concept. What both theorists posit is that people do not exist in a vacuum or in a silo devoid of context or reference points. Their ideas reassert the obvious point that while people are able to control some areas of their lives, there are, at the same time, many areas that affect them (directly and indirectly) over which they have little or no control. The key point is that despite their lack of direct contact with these areas, people are still affected and influenced by forces that are beyond their influence or control. Similarly, it would be a misrepresentation of the nature and the character of an individual if they are only defined according to just one aspect of their being. In other words, to think of an individual as a mere service user and not take account of other aspects of their identity is to view them through a very narrow lens. Similarly, seeing someone just as an ethnic minority, a lesbian or gay person, an asylum seeker, as middle-class, a Muslim or a traveller (Gypsy or Roma) is both reductive and a partial representation of the individual concerned. Engaging with anti-discriminatory practice requires honesty about one's prejudices and perhaps a reconsideration of one's views and beliefs about others.

KEY CONCEPTS

LANGUAGE USE

During the 1980s and 1990s, social work came in for a great deal of criticism and ridicule because of its focus on changing language use. Social work, in line with many local authorities, believed that what is said and how it is said (irrespective of the actual intention of the speaker), makes a difference in the perpetuation of discrimination in society and is a contributory factor in discriminatory practices. The view was that the way that language is used mattered because it is through language that people's attitudes and behaviour are shaped. The philosophical foundation of this assertion is evident in the works of Spender (1990) and Vygotsky (1986). In *Man Made Language*, Spender asserts that the English language is not gender neutral and as a result it is androcentric (male centred) in nature. Furthermore, she observed that 'One of the basic principles of feminism is that society has been constructed with bias which favours males; one of the basic principles of feminists who are concerned with language is that this bias can be located in the language' (Spender 1990: 14). Although Spender was primarily concerned with gender, other commentators have focused on the impact of language on race, culture and sexual orientation and impairment (Thompson 2003b; Kashima et al. 2008).

The assertion is that through language people are able to reinforce existing discriminatory attitudes and continue the marginalisation of certain groups in society. To redress the balance, many believed that by exorcising derogatory, offensive and discriminatory terms a great deal would be achieved in combating all forms of discrimination and discriminatory practices. So, as previously mentioned in Chapter 1, words that were once deemed acceptable (coloured, handicap, luv, dyke, queer and nigger) came under closer scrutiny and were found to be no longer appropriate or acceptable. Interestingly, at the same time as the purging of these terms was under way, there were radical groups who wanted to assert their right to exist alongside others. These movements believed that rather than be cowered or offended by the misrepresentation of their communities and the stereotyping of their identity, they would inject a more militant and confrontational approach by reclaiming and appropriating these offensive and derogative terms. For example, there were young black men who would often refer to themselves as niggers (with attitudes), gay men who called themselves queers (friends of Dorothy), lesbian women who were proud to be called dykes and some people with impairment using the term spastic and handicap. This approach was an attempt to turn negative terms on their head and confront the dehumanising prejudices inherent in these terms.

Anti-discriminatory practice requires practitioners to understand the importance of language use and the need to demonstrate sensitivity and awareness during interactions with people, irrespective of whether they are service users, other professionals or the general public (anti-discriminatory practice is not only implemented during working hours). It would not be controversial to suggest that language has the power to shape relationships because it frames the nature of the encounters (however long) between people. As Thompson (2003b) makes clear:

It is important to be aware that language is not simply the ability to use words to get across a particular message. Language actually runs much more deeply than this and refers to the complex array of interlocking relationships which forms the basis of communication and social interaction. Language is also a set of interlocking relationships in its own right, in the sense that meaning arises from the way in which particular language forms are combined and interact with one another. (2003b: 37)

Furthermore, 'Language is not simply a naturally occurring phenomenon, but rather is a complex system or, indeed, a set of systems which interlink with a range of social and psychological factors' (ibid.).

Thompson's analysis of language is both interesting and informative as he identifies the interactional and interlocking nature of language. In this context, the language that is used during the encounter between people could either reinforce (or perpetuate) existing biases and discriminatory practices, or it could be used in a way that demonstrates an acute understanding of its transformative character.

THE POWER OF COMMUNICATION

Communication is an important skill in social work and (with the fear of over exaggeration) it is effectively the life blood of the profession. It would be a mistake for a practitioner to believe that communication requires very little thinking and that no particular skills are necessary. Communication involves a complex web of thinking, actions and inter-action. It is not just about what is said and how it is said, it is also about the method by which information is communicated and how it is received. As Patni observed:

> At first encounter, communication conjures up notions of either written or verbal messages – handwritten, face-to-face, or technologically delivered messages through phone, email, and teleconferencing. However, we can convey love, disdain, hatred and passion through our eyes, our hands communicate in pointing and elaborating our verbal exchanges, our heads nod, our bodies communicate openness or distrust. Similarly our posture communicates submissiveness and dominance and our clothes, hair-styles, shoes and body piercing or tattooing also communicate. These serve as symbolic codes and often they deliver a message about our attitudes, opinions and choices and therefore have a communicative potential. (2008: 71)

Patni rightly observed that verbal exchanges are small parts of communication because of equal importance are the non-verbal signs. Unspoken communication includes nebulous concepts such as aura and physicality, the meaning ascribed to what is said, tonality, the perceived intention of the speaker, the interpretation of what is said by the listener and the omissions that hang in the air during an encounter. Anti-discriminatory practice recognises all these aspects of communication and, as a result, it requires practitioners to have a sharpened sense of awareness about themselves in all situations and encounters. This means that practitioners have to recognise, whatever their own position in society, that people who experience discrimination are sensitive about the views they believe others hold about them. They, therefore, look to see and try and get a sense of whether the practitioner understands 'where they are coming from' and whether the practitioner is attuned to or understands their experiences in society. However, it is worth reiterating the point that being sensitive and understanding of people's experience of discrimination does not mean that practitioners have to accept everything that is said to them. Or to allow discriminatory attitudes and beliefs that may be deemed acceptable in some other cultures and societies to go unchallenged. In fact, the opposite is the case in that anti-discriminatory practice encourages the challenging of negative, abusive and discriminatory attitudes and practices irrespective of the society or culture from which it emanates. The challenge for the practitioner is about demonstrating the skills of communicating and conveying social work intangibles such as genuineness, empathy, positive regard, respect and warmth.

ASSESSMENT

Assessment is one of the key areas of social work practice and it is often the starting point from which everything else flows. Assessment as Middleton asserted:

> In a social welfare context, … is a basis for planning what needs to be done to maintain or improve a person's situation. … Assessment involves gathering and interpreting information in order to understand a person and their circumstances; the desirability of change and the services and resources which are necessary to affect it. It involves making judgement based on information. (1997: 5)

In any intervention, it is perhaps in the area of assessment that evidence of bias and discrimination would first emerge. As Rees (1991) observed, assessment is not value-free and as such it is inevitable that practitioners will be influenced in the way they go about gathering information and conducting the assessment. The situation is even more acute with regard to risk assessment. As noted:

> The primary problem with risk assessment is that the information on which decisions must be based is usually inadequate. Because the decision cannot wait, the gaps in information must be bridged by inference and belief, and these cannot be evaluated in the same way as facts.

Improving the quality and comprehensiveness of knowledge is by far the most effective way to improve risk assessment. (National Research Council 1983 in Adams, 1995: 49)

It is sometimes implied that an affective assessment involves the practitioner starting with a clean slate and so not to be influenced by what may have gone before (Parker and Bradley 2003). While the sentiment behind this approach is understandable, the dangers are that practitioners are at a disadvantage. In our view, information is the lifeblood of the profession and lack of information does not enhance the quality of the work nor does it prevent discriminatory assumption and biases. The hallmark of a good social worker is not that they are devoid of information so as not to be influenced by what they may have read, but in fact they are able to look at the information available (with all its inaccuracies, assumptions, prejudices and biases) and assess it objectively and professionally.

The danger of the clean slate approach is that there is a disconnection and fragmentation between the past (what may have gone before), the present (how things are currently) and the future (what may happen in the future). There is almost an unchallengeable orthodoxy in social work that social workers should make judgements but must not be judgemental, that it is important not to impose one's values on others, that there are no right or wrong situations or good or bad values (Parker and Bradley 2003). To some extent, it is unfortunate that the social care and social work profession, in its attempt to be non-discriminatory in its approach, should have followed this line of thinking without closer scrutiny. The outcome has been that social workers have often gone against their 'gut feelings' in an effort not to appear oppressive or discriminatory. They have been paralysed to act in situations where they have observed conditions that were not just 'bad' but absolutely awful. They keep quiet when confronted with cultural and familial practices that, ordinarily, would have been deemed totally unacceptable. Findings from a range of social inquiries from Maria Colwell (1973); Stephen Meurs (1975); Neil Howlett (1976); Darren Clark (1979); Heidi Koseda (1984); Jasmine Beckford (1984); Tyra Henry (1984); Lauren Wright (2001); Kimberly Carlile (2003); Victoria Climbie (2005) and baby P (2009) have all, in their different ways, highlighted the dangers of treading too carefully in an effort not to upset or appear censorious towards service users. The misguided approach has damaged social work immeasurably and the fall-out from it has, in our view, sapped the confidence of the profession and its practitioners.

For example, in the Climbie case, one of the witnesses (Mr Graham) urged the inquiry to be 'alive to the possibility' that race may have influenced the approach taken in the case. Too often, in our view, social workers are blamed for inadequate assessment, poor responses and illogical judgement. Disapprobation is heaped on them for not doing their jobs properly because they appeared not to notice the obvious.

Despite its shortcomings, the 'rule of optimism', now perhaps misapplied within anti-discriminatory practice, still dominates the general approach in social work practice. This point is well captured in the Beckford inquiry when it observed that:

> Dingwall, Eeklaar and Murray, in their work, *The Protection of Children – State Intervention and Family Life* (1983) note the rarity of allegation by social workers of mistreatment of children by their parents. They describe this attitude as the product of the 'rule of optimism' that staff are required, if possible, to think the best of parents. The authors attribute this tendency in staff to two 'institutional devices' – namely (a) cultural relativism; and (b) natural love. The former is an intellectual position that all cultures are an equally valid way of formulating relationships between human beings and between human beings and the material world. Members of one culture 'have no right to criticise members of another by importing their own standards of judgement'. The latter is derived from the belief that parent/child life is 'an institutional phenomenon grounded in human nature'. If it is assumed that all parents love their children as a fact of nature, then it becomes very difficult to read evidence in a way which is inconsistent with this assumption. (Blom-Cooper 1985: 216).

Although in this case the reference is to race and culture, in the other cases mentioned earlier the focus is on other aspects. These aspects may relate to social class, poverty, drugs and alcohol misuse and poor living conditions and circumstances of the family or individuals concerned.

In our view, anti-discriminatory practice does not preclude being judgemental, setting out clear boundaries about acceptable behaviour, nor does it encourage a collapse into a relativistic morass of inactivity. As has already been discussed, anti-discriminatory practice is about making judgements, challenging discrimination and acknowledging that there is a requirement to be judgemental because some views, behaviours and attitudes are acceptable and others are not. This reinforces the point that anti-discriminatory practice is not just concerned with external factors such as structures, systems and processes, it is also concerned about interactions and people's conduct.

INTROSPECTIVE, REFLEXIVE AND REFLECTIVE PRACTICE

Our interpretation of anti-discriminatory practice is that it recognises that people do not exist in a vacuum and that although people may be influenced by their biases and prejudices, they are also capable of acting in a fair and just manner. So rather than 'pretending' that one is facing all situations tabula rasa, the key lies in the ability to be reflexive and reflective about one's practice. As already mentioned, anti-discriminatory practice is based on a philosophical underpinning that straddles a range of disciplines and practical social work skills.

Another area of skills and knowledge that would enhance anti-discriminatory practice is practitioners' ability to be introspective, reflexive and reflective about their practice. Higham opined that:

> Reflection can help students avoid a 'scatter gun' approach to theories and knowledge and begin to piece together the different strands of values, knowledge, and skills because sharing strategies for addressing issues can help to overcome stalemates in practice and frustrations arising from the difficult demanding nature of social work. (2006: 200)

In our view, it is not just students who would benefit from avoiding the scatter gun approach to theories and knowledge but all those involved in all areas of social care and social work would find the reflective approach a rewarding and effective way to practice.

Reflective practice is a range of ideas that have been developed to enable practitioners to be proactive in the way they engage with practice. Instead of viewing practice as a series of functions that have to be performed, they are expected to develop emotional intelligence and develop the ability to stand back and think about what they are doing. Using concepts such as introspection, reflexivity and reflectivity to develop the necessary self-awareness and enhanced practice evaluation, the general aim is to improve the way practitioners engage with their practice. *Introspection* requires the continual examination of one's thoughts, feelings and impressions. It is about the ability of the practitioner to understand that all actions have consequences (whether intended or not), and it is therefore both in their interest and in other people's interest that they give some consideration to their experiences in the situation and the motivation and driving force behind their actions. *Reflexivity* complements introspection in many ways in that it is about self-awareness and the ability to evaluate critically one's actions and take account of the influences on one's actions. So, for example, a reflexive approach would require a practitioner to think about and analyse how their own identity (race, class, sexual orientation, religion, gender) and personal circumstance impacted on their work and their approach. Similarly, *reflective practice* also builds on the practitioner's capacity to be conscious about and recognise themselves in the situation. Based on the work of Schön (1987), one of the ideas is that practitioners should think about what they are doing while they are doing it. An important area identified by Schön, which is of great relevance to anti-discriminatory practice, is the idea of reflection-inaction. The concept is a conscious process that requires challenging one's perception and assumptions.

Within the context of anti-discriminatory practice, what unites introspective, reflexive and reflective practice is the expectations that practitioners develop a consciousness about themselves in the situation. In other words, far from the physicality of doing the job, they also have to have a presence of mind about what they are doing, why they are doing it, what else they could do and what is influencing what they are doing. Unlike Adams, Dominelli and Payne (2002), we do not accept that these concepts are passive and that one only requires critical thinking in order to achieve the desired change. The tenets of introspective, reflexive and reflective practice are about questioning one's views and assumptions; it is about thinking, knowledge and understanding; it is about making sense of one's actions and reactions; it is about a deep sense of self-awareness; it is about scrutinising one's judgement. In our view, introspective, reflexive and reflective practice '*as it is*' (Adams, Dominelli and Payne 2002: 87) is the first step towards achieving transformation because it reinforces much of the knowledge and understanding that anti-discriminatory practice requires.

CONCLUSION

What we have tried to demonstrate is that anti-discriminatory practice requires a range of knowledge and skills in order to be effective. As well as knowledge of resources, human growth and development, impact of social policy and welfare, organisational systems, structures and processes, practitioners should also have a good understanding of their own prejudices, biases, feelings and views about others. Social work practitioners are often in a very uncomfortable place because on the one hand they are asked to make judgements and on the other hand they are schooled in not being judgemental or imposing their values on others. We however accept that there is of course a difference between making judgements and being judgemental. Practitioners know from their own (tacit knowledge) experiences that it is possible to develop a profile of the range of problems that are experienced by service users. They are also able to discern that there are certain similarities in people's situations, their conditions and in their reactions to their circumstances. Despite their knowledge and experience of these matters, practitioners try hard not to act on it because they are taught to be non-judgemental, to go into situations without preconceived ideas, not to look for similarities but almost to treat each situation they find themselves in as if it is unique. In our view, anti-discriminatory practice does not mean going into a place without any preconceptions. As we have tried to show, it is about looking beyond one's preconceptions and assumptions and having and using the necessary knowledge and skills to work in a way that does not discriminate.

Points to ponder

- Are there any particular skills and knowledge required in anti-discriminatory practice? If so, why are such skills and knowledge necessary?

It is acknowledged that assessment is not value-free and as such it is inevitable that practitioners will be influenced in the way they go about gathering information and conducting the assessment.

- But should practitioners embark on an assessment without any preconception, as a blank slate?
- What are the dangers of the 'rule of optimism'?
- Is there any distinction to be drawn between being judgemental and making judgement? If so, how would you characterise the difference?
- How is introspective, reflexive and reflective practice relevant to anti-discriminatory practice?

8

Integrating Anti-discriminatory Practice into Social Work Methods and Approaches

Introduction
Integrated approach
Key concepts
Crisis intervention
Task-centred approach
Cognitive-behavioural approach
Psychodynamic (psychoanalytical) approach
Conclusion

INTRODUCTION

This chapter attempts to integrate the methods and approaches utilised in social work with anti-discriminatory practice. Rather than rehearsing what is already known about the methods, the aim is to discuss and consider the applicability and integration of anti-discriminatory practice ideas in the different methods and approaches generally used in social work. Social work has worked very hard in developing a professional approach. Although it works with abstract concepts and ideas, it is also interested in evidence-based practice. Like anti-discriminatory practice, the method and approaches that social work rely on is a fusion of different theories and ideas. These theories were developed not only to give an air of professionalism and legitimacy to the social work profession, although this in itself is important, but to also give the profession and practitioners a set of tools with which to ply their trade.

Dealing with people's problems and trying to encourage people to take control of their lives could not only be left to chance, good intentions and common sense. People are shaped by a myriad of influences and for a practitioner, understanding what those influences are and what form they take and what part they play in people's day-to-day lives is important. Just as crucial is the need for practitioners to acquire general knowledge and appropriate skills that encourage and facilitate change. Developing the necessary skills and acquiring the appropriate knowledge could make a difference between a successful intervention and one that is based on mere hunches, although we would submit that hunches, common sense, instincts and 'gut feeling' also have their role to play in practice (Okitikpi and Aymer 2008).

INTEGRATED APPROACH

Anti-discriminatory practice should not be viewed as a bolt-on to the practice of social work, nor should it not be considered as something that is separate to day-to-day practice that could only be afforded when time permits. We would suggest that anti-discriminatory practice is pivotal to social work because it provides the value base as well as the ethical and socio-political foundation upon which intervention is built. In addition to encouraging people to develop a greater sense of awareness of diversity and difference, it is an approach that requires practitioners to think widely about the range of influences on the lives of service users (see Figure 8.1 below).

In our view, anti-discriminatory practice encourages both a reflective and critical approach to practice. Reflective in that it requires the practitioner to stand back and consider how their views, attitudes (including their assumptions and expectations) and approach impacts on the service user and the work undertaken. Critical in that it recognises the dynamic nature of the relationship between competing factors (service users' experiences and their needs, practitioners' outlook and their approach, resource availability, the impact and influences of social structures and organisation systems), and the existence of the power imbalance between those involved.

Practitioners are acutely aware of the complexities of power, particularly the affect and impact of the power dynamics between themselves and service users. However, they are also aware from their practice experiences that power is not a lineal concept. For example, they would be able to attest to the fact that although they are, by dint of their professional role, in a powerful position compared to a service user, this does not mean that they necessarily hold power *over* that service user.

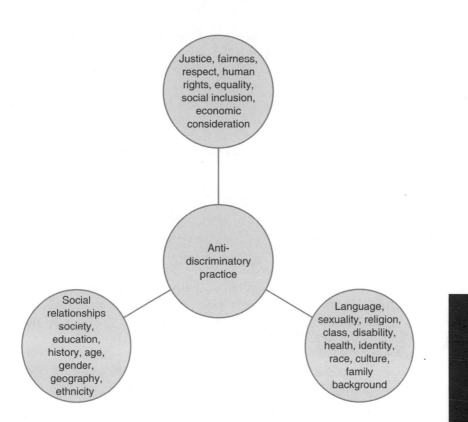

Figure 8.1   Influences

KEY CONCEPTS

CRISIS INTERVENTION

Crisis intervention is built on the premise that people are likely to change during a period of crisis. The rationale being that faced with a crisis, people have very few options but to search for a way to resolve the problem. However, if having exhausted their coping strategies they are still unable to resolve the situation, then they are more susceptible to new ideas or suggestions from others. The assertion is that people are generally influenced by their experiences and their aim is to find a solution in order to regain the balance in their life. The approach recognises that people are prone to treating their experiences of discomfort or stressful situation as a crisis. As the approach tries to make clear, not every difficult event or stressful situation should be described as a crisis. The skill lies in the practitioner's ability to stand back and ensure that what is happening is a genuine crisis. It may of course be the case that the service user experiences their situation as a crisis while the practitioner may view the situation differently. While it is important for the practitioner to work with the reality of the service user and not dismiss their feelings and experience as unreasonable or irrational, they nevertheless have to refrain from getting into a crisis themselves. Their role is to remain focused, bring calmness into the situation and understand how to work with the approach in order to encourage and facilitate change. Unlike a lay person's understanding of crisis, in this approach, crisis is defined as 'an upset in a steady state' (Rapoport 1970: 276). Based on the work of Caplan (1964), the approach suggests that people exist in a steady state or equilibrium (or homeostasis) and all efforts are made to keep within this balance. As people live their lives, difficulties and problems they encounter on a day-to-day basis are dealt with using their habitual (normal) coping mechanism. Crisis occurs when people's coping mechanisms or their 'habitual strengths for coping do not work: we fail to adjust either because the situation is new to us, or it has not been anticipated or a series of events becomes too overwhelming' (Coulshed 1988: 68). Coulshed (1988) observed that Caplan (1964) highlighted that there are four phases involved in a crisis and these are characterised as:

1. There is a rise in tension in response to a stress or events. Habitual problem-solving mechanisms are called upon to preserve the steady state.
2. A further rise in tension and disorganisation occurs as the individual (or system) avoids doing anything or makes desperate attempts to cope.
3. Inner and outer resources are put into action and some kind of resolution reached, but this may be incomplete or lead to diminished problem-solving in the future.
4. Beyond this, personality and behaviour can become so disorganised that a 'nervous breakdown' occurs. There could be magical thinking such as 'if I don't think about it, the problem will disappear', a retreat into fantasy and a loss of touch with reality.

(1988: 41)

It is during these phases that the practitioner has a good chance of instigating change. The approach recognises that people cannot be in a permanent state of crisis so there is a set limit of time, judged to be about six weeks, by which any effective work has to be completed. Ultimately, the aim is to restore coping capacity and re-ignite the ability to deal with problems as they present themselves. As identified by Trevithick, the approach:

> draws from psychoanalytical theory, particularly ego psychology, and emphasis that people's capacity to deal with problems ... is based on three factors: people's internal psychological strengths and weakness (ego strength); the nature of the problem being faced and the quality of the help being given. (2000: 184)

In crisis intervention, there is a possibility that the practitioner may need to take charge of the situation as a means of helping the service user to regain their coping capacity and their strengths. In our view, taking charge of a crisis situation and placing the user's involvement on hold need not, and indeed should not, be viewed negatively. Anti-discriminatory practice does not preclude practitioners using their knowledge, experience and expertise to alleviate a crisis situation. Indeed, we would argue that it would be a dereliction of duty to insist on a service user finding their own solution to their problems. If they were able to resolve the situation before it became a crisis, they would not have needed help or requested social work intervention. It is worth keeping a clear perspective on these matters.

Crisis intervention takes account of both the internal and external factors that may have triggered the crisis. Working within an Anti-discriminatory practice framework would require that the practitioner provide the necessary stabilising effect while at the same time taking into consideration (during the assessment phase) the history and personal biography of the individual or family concerned. In other words, being a service user is just one label that is applicable to the individual/family – there are other categorisations and labels as well. Seeking out a more holistic picture through a better understanding of people's biography may hold the key to working with people's strengths rather than only with their weaknesses. For example, because a person is in crisis and their habitual coping mechanism is not working and they have become overwhelmed by their situation, it should not be read that they are therefore devoid of personality and identity. In such instances, anti-discriminatory practice would require the worker to maintain respect, focusing on stabilising the situation (including taking control as needs be), and helping to restore the person's strengths and coping skills. An anti-discriminatory practice with this model requires both a practical and psychological response. For example, as well as triggering the practical help and support that would be needed in such a situation, the practitioner would also need to keep at the forefront of their mind the realities of people's experience. So personal biography in terms of identity (gender, race, class, sexual orientation, religion and other areas) are as important a consideration as the crisis itself. An anti-discriminatory practice approach would not fail to consider the possibility that people's crisis situation may have been triggered because of their background or their sense of identity or because of their position in society. In addition, enabling people to regain their emotional and psychological strength in order to achieve homeostasis may in fact require taking a broader outlook. This may mean, in some cases, enabling or reconnecting people to (or not) their background. Also, how people cope with their situation or the crisis they may be experiencing may be inextricably linked to their background and their identity. Within the context of anti-discriminatory practice, such possibilities should not be left to chance nor considered as secondary. Rather, they would be regarded as important factors that may help in the stabilisation of the situation.

TASK-CENTRED APPROACH

The task-centred approach is often teamed with crisis intervention and it is easy to see why this should be the case. As explained above, crisis intervention is used to stabilise a situation that has deteriorated. However, having calmed the situation and regained some kind of equilibrium, the next stage would be to consolidate effectively whatever gains have been achieved. Task-centred work holds that people are capable of making the necessary long-term changes in their lives if they are supported and given clear guidance. One of the core principles of the approach is the view that it is not possible to facilitate change if the person, who after all is the focus of the change, has not been involved in setting the agenda or contributing to the whole process. This method is a partnership-based approach that envisages a close working relationship between the practitioner and the service user. It is a relatively brief, time-limited approach, with 12 interviews over a three to four month period, and focuses on set goals. Based on the work of Reid and Epstein (1972), the approach could be used in at least eight different practice areas. These include:

- interpersonal conflict
- problems with formal organisations
- reactive emotional distress
- dissatisfaction in social relations
- problems in social transition
- difficulties in role performance
- behavioural problems
- inadequate resources.

The uniqueness of the task-centred approach is that it breaks down the difficulties and problems into small, and ultimately manageable, components. The approach involves the practitioner and the service user identifying the main problem(s) and then working out how to reformulate them into easily manageable practical tasks. Once the tasks have been agreed, the next stage is to divide the tasks between the practitioner and the service user and then decide who is going to work on which task and over what period. It is an approach that compels the practitioner and the service user to look very closely at the presenting problem(s) and reformulate them into a range of small practical tasks. The work involves identifying specific steps that would need to be undertaken in order to achieve the agreed set tasks. It is important to note that it is not just a case of meeting with the service user and setting randomly agreed goals. In this approach, the practitioner has practical duties to perform as well providing support and encouraging the service user to carry out the mutually agreed tasks. The process involved in developing the goals entails five phases:

1. Exploring the problems – this involves discussing the problem(s) honestly and explicitly. It is about clarification and understanding the nature and depth of the problem(s). It is important at this stage to highlight (all) the problems and for the service user to rank them into what they consider to be the order of importance.
2. Setting out the objective – it is during this phase that the problem is broken down into practical and manageable tasks. The aim is to ensure that the tasks are concrete rather than abstract and there is an agreed criteria for measuring whether it has been done or not. During this phase, the problem needs to be matched to any one of the eight areas identified.
3. Working out an agreement (written or verbal) – this sets out the duties and obligations on the practitioner and the service user. It should also set out the frequency of meetings, the location and the duration.

4. The approach (achieving the objective) – how the tasks that have been agreed are going to be carried out and achieved is open for discussion.
5. Ending – this phase is just as important as the other four phases and should be built into the approach from the beginning. The practitioner and the service user should have an idea when the work will end and there should be opportunity and time set aside to evaluate their achievements.

Unlike crisis intervention, there is no theoretical framework that informs the task-centred approach. Rather, there is an implicit assumption that change is more likely to occur and be lasting when people are given the opportunity to be actively involved in finding a workable and realistic solution. Integrating anti-discriminatory practice in the task-centred approach means not seeing the problems in isolation but understanding that backgrounds do affect the way people view their problems. For example, in some cultures, reactive emotional distress is manifested in physical terms rather than psychologically, emotionally or through experiencing depression. Understanding the service user's background and taking time to discover the nature of their experiences (in addition to the problems) could make a difference at the initial stages of the approach. Those who have experience of discrimination tend to be wary of others and they look for signals (generally verbal, but often non-verbal) that reassure them that the person dealing with them and their family understands and appreciates their particular experience in society. Task-centred is essentially an empowering approach that believes in the capabilities and capacities of the service user to achieve change. One of the key aspects of anti-discriminatory practice is the recognition of the impact of discrimination, poverty, injustices, inequalities and unfairness on people's lives. Being able to understand the relationship between these socio-political realities and the problems as identified by the service user would be an important anti-discriminatory stance. This of course does not mean an unqualified acceptance of what is presented by the service user because the worker does have a role in filtering (see Chapter 10) people's description or explanation of their situation. The challenge for both the practitioner and the service user would be how to turn the identified areas into practical goals and steps to be worked on. The power differentiation between the practitioner and the service user does not disappear, and indeed we would argue that it would be a false premise and misleading to suggest there could ever be a situation whereby the practitioner and the service user have equal power in the relationship.

The task-centred approach dovetails very well with anti-discriminatory practice in this regard because it encourages the practitioner to do what they do best and that is to bring their *expertise* into the relationship and work on tasks alongside the service user. The aim is to support (and therefore maximise the chances of success), and facilitate change through being an enabler. The core aspects of the task-centred approach that include working in partnership, collaboration, working with service users' strengths, building on confidence, systemic and responsive communication are, in our view, the same core elements that characterise anti-discriminatory practice.

COGNITIVE-BEHAVIOURAL APPROACH

The cognitive-behavioural approach has a long pedigree in probation and social work practice, particularly in working with young people, adults, offenders and in youth work, residential units and daycare practices. The approach is still popular because of the fact that practitioners are able to easily grasp the core principle of the method. Although it is quite a complex approach to fully put into operation, the underlying theory is not too complicated. One of the strengths of the approach is that people are able to observe from their own personal experiences how the approach works or could work. Briefly, without getting into the history of how behaviourism and cognitive theory came to be amalgamated to form the cognitive-behavioural approach, the starting point is that human behaviour and attitudes are shaped by a combination of external and internal influences. The external consideration, primarily based on the work of learning theorists, asserts that behaviour is shaped by the constant interaction between the person and their environment. As Medcof and Roth observed: 'you enter the world with a genetic potential that contributes to your ultimate patterns of adjustment. But learning and experience also determine the kind of person you become' (1979: 106). The internal considerations work from the premise that human beings are not passive puppets that are only shaped by their environment. On the contrary, there is an interplay and interconnection between the environment and the internal organising processes that make up the human form. So, according to Medcof and Roth:

The cognitive approach emphasises the role of mediation processes in human behaviour. These internal processes affect behaviour at several levels, including (a) learning and storing facts (b) solving problems and communicating with others, and (c) maintaining self consistency and defining one's feelings. (1979: 182)

As a combined method, the cognitive-behavioural approach offers the opportunity for the practitioner and the service user to address not just the behaviour but also the cognition, views and attitudes that are linked to the behaviour. So, of interest would be the cognitive processes and rationale that were antecedents and contributory to the behaviour. Unlike many of the other approaches, the cognitive-behavioural approach is not particularly interested in either the history of the problem or in providing a justification for the problem; rather it focuses on the here and now and looks for ways to change maladaptive behaviour. It is a brief, highly focused, systematic and structured approach that would work with the service user and, if needs be, the significant others in their lives. There are of course different adaptations of the cognitive-behavioural approach, but it could be argued that they are all based on a combination of ideas and variations of the classical behavioural techniques (operant conditioning, aversion therapy, modelling and desensitisation, social learning theory, action therapy) and various cognitive therapy models (cognitive restructuring, guided self-change, motivation work and assertiveness training).

Interestingly, there is an element of task-centred approach in the cognitive-behavioural approach, especially where there are clearly identified tasks and goals to be achieved. It is important to note that the cognitive-behavioural approach is not just pure behaviourism with a light cognitive touch or vice versa. This is a method that requires clear assessment and a carefully formulated plan of intervention as well as a formula for monitoring and evaluating the intervention. Although the practitioner is quite directive in this method, there is, nevertheless, an expectation of a high level of involvement and input from the service user and significant others, since it is they who would have to carry out whatever work has been agreed.

There is an assumption that anti-discriminatory practice is a passive, woolly, utopian ideal that is more useful as a philosophical underpinning concept rather than something that could be practically applied. We believe that while it is the case that anti-discriminatory practice is informed by philosophical ideals and ethos, there are nevertheless practical dimensions to the concept. So, for example, a cognitive-behavioural approach encourages the practitioner to see the service user as a whole person rather than just as a problem. In this approach, the focus is on finding a solution to the problem instead of labelling or demonising the service user. The early stages of the approach demand that the practitioner gets a good understanding of the problem. The extent to which a service user would feel comfortable enough to discuss their problems openly and honestly with a practitioner who is 'different' from themselves is dependent on the kind of relationship that is able to be developed between them. The approach is complex because it does not ignore the fact that people are complicated and that they live complicated lives. But rather than focusing merely on the complications and the intricacies of a service user's life, the aim is to turn thoughts, feelings and actions into clearly stated and identifiable behaviours that would then be the main focus for change. Because the emphasis is on the 'here and now' and the need to get a clear idea of the nature of the problem, the practitioner would have to be able to display practical anti-discriminatory practice skills such as:

- Communication skills at a much deeper level than perhaps may ordinarily be the case – these include understanding verbal and non-verbal communication, awareness of the posture that is adopted and being attuned to the 'vibes' or aura that is radiated.
- Listening skills – active listening, understanding what is meant.
- Language use – what is said, how it is said, what is meant.
- Non-prejudicial attitude – also linked to language because views and attitudes affect language which in turn influence behaviour.

One of the key features of the cognitive-behavioural approach is the recognition that the practitioner not only needs to be directive but there may also be a need, when necessary, to inject pedagogic elements to their approach. On the face of it, this may seem paradoxical to the aims and ethos of anti-discriminatory practice. In fact, our interpretation of anti-discriminatory practice is that it is not an unbridled laissez-faire concept in which self-determination and being an enabler mean non-directiveness or minimal contact. As already mentioned, anti-discriminatory practice, in our analysis, does not mean service users should be left to fend for or find the solution to their own problems themselves. Rather, we would suggest that anti-discriminatory practice, like the cognitive-behavioural approach, is an active concept and requires practitioners to have a heightened sense of awareness about the situation they are in.

PSYCHODYNAMIC (PSYCHOANALYTICAL) APPROACH

While it may be argued that the cognitive-behavioural approach lacks a single theoretical base, the same could not be said of the psychodynamic (psychoanalytical) approach. Despite the massive changes that have occurred in social work practice with the move away from long-term intervention towards brief, time-limited and target-orientated practice culture, the psychodynamic approach still enjoys a great deal of support within the profession. The advocates of the approach may argue that one of the reasons for its endurance, in spite of the pressures to conform to a limited intervention agenda, is because of the fact it has an internal logic and coherence that has proved difficult to dislodge. The approach originated from the work of Freud and was further developed by others (Bowlby 1951; Erikson 1965; Ainsworth et al. 1978; Hollis and Woods 1981; Klein 1984; Lacan 2008). Its starting point is that human beings are essentially shaped by intra-psychic dynamics (id, ego and super ego) which are located in their minds. It is the interaction and relationship between these internal elements and the immediate familial figures that makes a difference in the development of human beings. The theory behind the approach postulates that human development occurs in stages and each stage brings with it opposing pressures. These pressures or drives (instincts) need to be adequately addressed and the appropriate relief sought in order to avoid people being stuck at a stage or having difficulties either at the next stage or later on in life. One of the key features of the psychodynamic approach is the basic principle that all behaviours could be traced back to early childhood experiences. The core elements of the psychodynamic approach include concepts such as: the unconscious; psychic determinism; resistance; repression; attachment; ego psychology; regression; defence mechanism; transference; counter-transference; fixation; object relation; projection; splitting; rationalisation and sublimation.

The psychodynamic approach starts from the premise that it would be difficult to enable or facilitate change without any exploration of early childhood experiences. It is through gaining an understanding of early childhood events and relationships with key figures that one could begin to address the presenting problems. Also important is the nature and quality of the relationship between the individual and significant others. According to the doctrine, just teaching people to change their behaviour without getting them to develop insight into the cause of that behaviour is at best to paper over the cracks and at worst to make the condition chronic and more difficult to change.

It is important to recognise that psychodynamic theory has not remained static from its original inception. As observed by Payne:

> Modern psychoanalytic theory has moved away from the idea of drives as the basic influence on behaviour (Lowenstein 1985). It is more concerned with how individuals interact with their social world; it has become more social than biological. (2005: 78)

Despite Payne's assertion, one of the criticisms levelled towards the psychodynamic approach is that it is only interested in the experiences of individuals and their particular biography. More crucially, it is suggested that the approach takes very little account of external factors such as the extent of cultural, social and environmental influences on people's lives (Trevithick 2000). It is also suggested that it is too inward looking because it focuses on intra-psychic and interpersonal relationships, perhaps to the detriment of other important areas.

One of the great misapprehensions about the psychodynamic approach is that it is essentially a model that is best suited to rich, middle-class white people. The reason for this accusation is best illustrated by Trevithick (2000: 187) who pointed out that, 'As a therapy [psychodynamic], it is elitist, expensive to access and lacks clear time boundaries. As a theory, its concepts are difficult to grasp ... psychoanalytical perspectives have been accused of being out of touch with bread and butter issues'.

It is unfortunate that the approach should be saddled with such historical baggage because it is an approach that is applicable to all service user groups, irrespective of their backgrounds. As already discussed in this chapter, anti-discriminatory practice is as much about individuals as it is about wider considerations. Enabling people to gain an insight into their intra-psychic and interpersonal relationships does not diminish the centrality of anti-discriminatory practice. Applying anti-discriminatory practice in this instance involves, interestingly, paying close attention to the interaction between the service user and their familial environment, including the nature of the interpersonal relationship between those concerned. In addition, just as psychoanalytical perspective is interested in transference and counter-transference between the service users and the practitioner, anti-discriminatory practice is also interested in the way the worker and the service user navigate their differences and how it may impact on their relationship.

The psychodynamic approach thrives on the trust relationship that is nurtured and maintained throughout the sessions. Like anti-discriminatory practice, it is an approach that takes great pride in not judging people negatively on the basis of differences. Instead, it attempts to provide an opportunity for people to express their pains, anger, frustrations, unhappiness, hopes and dreams. It sees people holistically rather than as fragmented, distorted or compartmentalised beings. Importantly, it works hard to keep a neutral position irrespective of external pressure to attach negative labels on people. So at a glance it is evident that Anti-discriminatory practice and the psychodynamic approach have much in common. A practitioner attempting to integrate anti-discriminatory practice with this approach would need to take account of difference and consider the extent to which 'difference' impacts and contributes to the service user's situation. Furthermore, they would have to be able to reflect on how their differences with the service user either facilitate or get in the way of a productive and successful professional and constructive relationship. As well as developing a high level of awareness of how discriminations are manifested, the practical aspects of anti-discriminatory practice, in this particular approach, may involve investigating and understanding the backgrounds of the service user, both in terms of the individual's personal history but also with regard to the communities with which they identify. The reasons for this are twofold: firstly, it would reinforce the holistic nature of the approach and secondly, it would enable the practitioner to develop a greater level of knowledge and insight of the world of the service user and the communities they may belong to. For example, working with a Nigerian, a Chinese, a Bulgarian, a Pakistani, a Jamaican or a South Vietnamese service user would require more than just knowing about their individual biographies. Understanding their communities could enhance the work undertaken and provide additional insight into their views of the world. This of course does not encourage cultural absolutism but it recognises that early childhood experiences are shaped by the myths, stories and community machinations that help bind groups together. In this example, cross-cultural considerations could impact on the approach that may be adopted.

CONCLUSION

This chapter has briefly attempted to discuss a number of social work methods and approaches with the aim of examining how anti-discriminatory concepts and ideas could be integrated into day-to-day practice. As already mentioned, anti-discriminatory practice is considered an integral part of good social work practice. But, as we have also discussed, implementing or incorporating anti-discriminatory concepts and ideas into one's everyday practice is not necessarily as easy as it is generally assumed. One of the difficulties for practitioners is that they often have to work under a tremendous amount of pressure and at such times it is very difficult for them to keep theories and concepts at the forefront of their minds all of the time. In addition, practitioners may have to work with hostile service users who have no intention of cooperating with them or helping to find appropriate solutions to their identified problems.

Points to ponder

- How does power difference affect the relationship between practitioners and service users?
- Consider the assertion that practitioners have power over all service users.
- How important is it for practitioners to explore difference with service users? Would such exploration foster a better working relationship?
- What are the key skills necessary to integrate anti-discriminatory practice into social work methods?
- What are the key ideas that connect anti-discriminatory practice and social work methods?

ADP and social work

9
The Dynamic Nature of Anti-discriminatory Practice

Introduction
Unintended consequences of ADP
Key concepts
Children's services
Adult services
Disability
Mental health
Community development
Conclusion

INTRODUCTION

This chapter provides a brief reflection on some of the material already discussed in this book and highlights the complex and dynamic nature of anti-discriminatory practice. The emphasis throughout this book has been to encourage practitioners to be less defensive in their approach and to foster the necessary confidence to challenge (in a constructive and empowering way) discriminatory practices. Focusing on some of the service areas, for example, children and families; adult services; disability; mental health and community development, the aim is to acknowledge the changes that continue to take place in these areas of work. It is also to highlight the importance of developing a general understanding of the underlying issues involved in working in these areas and to think about the application of anti-discriminatory practice in a changing practice environment.

It almost seems perverse to some people that in the 21st century there is still a need to be arguing the case for maintaining momentum on anti-discriminatory practice. For many practitioners, and service users,

key concepts in
anti-discriminatory social work

126

the aims and objectives of the concept appear to be not only right and just but it would indeed seem strange and irrational to argue for the opposite. After all, who would want to suggest that black and Southern Asian people, by dint of their racial and cultural backgrounds, are intellectually and culturally inferior and not as capable as white people. Even those who are on the extreme right of the political spectrum now couch their arguments about the perceived differences between black and white people on 'cultural' incompatibility rather than advancing the superiority and inferiority debate. On gender, it would again seem strange to suggest that in all spheres of life women are not as capable as men and that their place in the world is effectively secondary to that of men. We would suggest that even misogynistic and endocentric men would have to refuse to accept the evidence around them in order to maintain such a stance. Similarly, viewing disability as some kind of curse and homosexuality as an abomination and an act against human nature would require, in our view, some kind of intellectual somersault and the maintenance of what could only be described as a medieval and digressive world view about human beings.

As we have been at pains to point out, anti-discriminatory practice is about human rights, social justice and equality for all. The concept was born out of immense political struggle and some of the hard-won freedoms are now entrenched in various legislation. Ultimately, anti-discriminatory practice is about the right to self-determination through the removal of oppressive and discriminatory obstacles, be it social, cultural, religious, gender, age, sexuality, economic or political. Despite the enactment of various legislations and a progressive changing social landscape, there continues to be major concerns about discrimination in society. Why should this still be case and why is it important to continue to revisit it?

The gains made in developing anti-discriminatory practice should not be underestimated nor taken for granted. The idea was that no one should be treated unfairly because of his or her identity, cultural background, sexual orientation, social group membership, disability, religious beliefs or political leanings. At the outset, the overriding imperative was to highlight the unjust and negative experiences of those at the receiving end of discrimination. The next phase was to challenge the rights and power of those who regarded themselves as the arbiters of the mainstream and arbiters of societal knowledge, norms, values, mores and culture. It is no longer an exaggeration to suggest that anti-discriminatory ideas and policies now permeate society and social interactions to such an extent that many of the attitudes and behaviours that are now taken for granted owe much to the concept. For example, there is now a widespread recognition that language is not value free. As a result of this recognition, language use in society, in general, is tempered by an awareness of the danger of using terms that some may find offensive and discriminatory. So, for example, racist, sexist, homophobic or disabilist terms have come under intense scrutiny and people are unafraid to challenge negative and abusive terms. Similarly, broadcasters and media organisations are under obligation to consider the nature and contents of their medium and to ensure that they do not incite or promote discrimination. It is evident that television producers, film directors and theatre productions all make a great deal of effort not to be offensive or abusive towards different groups in society. The only area of exception to the rule of 'knowingly' causing offence and inciting discrimination is in the music industry. In this industry, there are musicians whose lyrics (some reggae artists are prone to homophobic lyrics, some hip-hop artist lyrics are misogynistic and there are also white supremacist bands) are not only offensive but the musicians positively glorify in the notoriety that their words generate. However, these artists and their genre of music face censorship from a sizeable number of people in society. In essence, the challenge to blatant racist, sexist and homophobic lyrics could be regarded as a testament to the penetration of Anti-discriminatory ideas and policies in society. It has made it more difficult for the kind of crude discriminatory practices and attitudes that were endemic prior to the struggles of the 1960s, 1970s, 1980s and 1990s to continue unchallenged.

UNINTENDED CONSEQUENCES OF ADP

It is important to acknowledge that as a result of the success that has been achieved in challenging all forms of discriminations, it is worthwhile considering some of the unforeseen consequences. The point of highlighting the unforeseen consequence is not to blame the victim or give ammunition to opponents of anti-discriminatory policies and practices. Rather, the reason is to be honest about all aspects of the working of the concept in order to ensure that the concept is reclaimed and its aims and objectives protected and reinforced. For example, we believe there has often been a misunderstanding or a misrepresentation of some aspects of anti-discriminatory practice. As already mentioned, anti-discriminatory practice was developed to challenge discriminations and to ensure that there was equal access and equal opportunities for all irrespective of backgrounds. It was never intended that it would support discrimination (homophobia, racism, disabilism, sexism, ageism, religious intolerance); ignore bad behaviour or attitudes; protect poor practitioners from censure; give solace to bigots; take no account of capabilities and abilities; turn interview sessions into farcical pantomimes (where known poor practitioners are interviewed just because they meet, on paper, the person specification); condone a worker refusing to work with certain groups because of their religious beliefs or a male Muslim dentist refusing to treat Muslim women who do not cover their head. In addition, as a result of the misinterpretation of the concept, any suggestions that did not champion the causes of disadvantaged groups, irrespective of their nature, were often deemed to be discriminatory. For example, encouraging non-English speakers who live in the country to speak English was considered discriminatory. It was asserted, with some force, that society should accommodate non-English speakers by providing interpreters and the translation of documents in as many languages as is spoken in the community. Similarly, encouraging the ethnic minority population in society to integrate was also viewed as discriminatory because it requires the ethnic minority population to adapt and acculturate into mainstream society. Finally, it was considered racist (in some quarters) to encourage, and indeed champion, 'British values' among all people who live in the country, irrespective of their cultural backgrounds.

While there may well be a cogent explanation and justification for accepting and championing each of the examples given above, the issue for consideration is the extent to which anti-discriminatory practice is interpreted as encouraging a separatist and sectarian (cultural and racial parallel) society whose only concern is just the minority population and the disadvantaged in society. We would argue that anti-discriminatory practice is a far more complex and dynamic concept. While it does indeed champion and defend the rights of the disadvantaged and those who are discriminated against, it does not do so at the expenses of others. Anti-discriminatory practice is as concerned about community, social and societal cohesion as it is about individual and groups rights.

KEY CONCEPTS

CHILDREN'S SERVICES

Rightly, in our view, the child's interest should always be considered as paramount and all work concerning children should have this mantra as the guiding principle. Too often, as identified in many of the public enquiries (Jasmine Beckford, Victoria Climbe, Tyra Henry, Baby Peter), the focus is often on trying to placate the children's parents or carers rather than concentrating on the needs and experiences of the child or children in the family. There is, understandably, a link between being non-judgemental and anti-discriminatory practice. Both encourage a way of working that humanises the service users and treats them with respect and maintains their dignity. Anti-discriminatory practice is an approach that transcends stereotypical assumptions. Unsurprisingly, the concept does not discriminate between people and therefore does not value one particular group over others. As a starting point, with regard to children's services, anti-discriminatory practice does not, in our view, subordinate the values, norms and expectations of the wider society in which the child lives to that of the child's family background. Effective anti-discriminatory practice requires some understanding of the child's family background. This should be viewed as part of building a profile of the child's history and circumstance, but not at the expense of individualising the child. Good practice demands assessment and investigation of the child's current situation, their circumstance as well as their history. Goodyer (2008) rightly observed that assessment is an important element of social work intervention and it can have a profound effect on the lives of children. Crisp et al. (2003) identified six main purposes of assessment and these are to:

- determine need
- consider eligibility for services
- consider suitability of carers or services
- facilitate decision-making
- contribute to multi-disciplinary assessments
- assess risk.

It is also at this early stage that discriminatory practices, either wittingly or by omission, become evident. It becomes evident in the way the assessment is carried out, the language used, the assumptions made about the child and their family, the lack of rigour in assessing the child and their family, the stereotyping of the child's family background and the bias and prejudicial way in which services and provisions are offered as well as the type of service given.

It is all about the child and their particular family

It would be unrealistic to expect practitioners to work with children and their families as if they are not part of a wider community. Indeed, service users are categorised according to set groupings. For example, reference is made to Afro-Caribbean children and their families, African children and their families, Asian children and their families, Traveller's children and their families, Polish children and their families, children of mixed parentage and their families, etc. etc. These cultural or ethnic categorisations often form the starting point from which everything else flows. In our view, the important point is that, while these categorisations are helpful in identifying the background of the child and their families, they are not enough to explain the totality of the child and their families. Working within the framework of anti-discriminatory practice requires a more circumspect approach and it should not be assumed that the child's family background could be so neatly identified or categorised. There are often as many variations within cultures and ethnic groups as there are between different cultures.

For example, how one white person defines being white may be different to the way others may define it. Similarly, one black or Asian person's definition of being their colour may be different to others. However, if one asked the question, what does it mean to be black or Asian in society? then the response may well be more straightforward. The reason this question is easier to address is partly due to the fact that there are reference points that people are able to call upon. This relates to the individual's experience of living in a predominately white society and their particular story of the way they are treated. However, stories about discrimination and racism are not the only way we would define black or Asian identity. The reason for making the point is that, in our view, anti-discriminatory practice with children and families needs to enable the children and their families to redevelop and 'rewrite' their own identity (scripts), without preconceptions. It should not be assumed that because they come from a particular background and community that they necessarily conform (or indeed want to) to the norms and values of that community. The other difficulty with such broad characterisation is that it treats everyone from the same ethnic or cultural background as if they are all the same, with shared values, aspirations and outlook in life. In other words, there is little consideration given to differences such as class, ethnicity, language, regionalism and political beliefs.

Anti-discriminatory practice matters to all

It is often the case that discussions about anti-discriminatory practice generally make little or no reference to white children and their families, except in the context of their discriminatory attitudes and beliefs. We believe this omission is a grave mistake as it reinforces the notion that discriminatory matters only relate to 'others' who are non-white. In our view, many white children and their families face as many difficulties and problems as others and their needs are just as important as other children and their families. As we have tried to emphasise throughout this publication, our interpretation of anti-discriminatory practice is that the concept is as concerned about minorities as it is about the majority population.

ADULT SERVICES

We would argue that there are essentially two dimensions to Anti-discriminatory practice. One dimension encourages practitioners to challenge discrimination in all its forms and not to treat people in a way that reinforces whatever discrimination they may already have experienced in society. The other dimension is that, irrespective of people's views, background or beliefs, they should be treated with respect and provided with equal opportunities and given equal access to services and provisions. In our view, while practitioners have been very good at adhering to the first dimension, they have often found it difficult dealing with the second. For example, there was a period when many practitioners refused to work with some individuals because they were deemed to be racists, sexists, homophobic or disabilist. Indeed, at one point, the National Probation Officers had a policy of not working with racially motivated offenders and local authority offices had signs in the public reception areas of their offices making it clear that verbal or physical abuse together with racist, sexist, homophobic or disabilist comments would not be tolerated. Of course, it is right that violence, aggression and discriminative, abusive remarks should not have to be endured by staff. An organisation not only has a duty to make their position clear to the public, but it also has a duty to protect its staff. The difficulty for staff is that, while it is appropriate to challenge discriminatory attitudes and behaviours, they also have to be able to work with the difficulty that is involved and try and provide an appropriate and non-discriminatory service to all. According to our interpretation, anti-discriminatory practice, as we have already mentioned, does not discriminate between people, rather it accepts diversity and differences. It is a concept that believes that it is important to see beyond the assumption and labelling and treat everyone in a non-discriminatory manner.

What this means in practice when working with adults with discriminatory attitudes is that the practitioners not only have to appropriately challenge such negative attitudes and behaviours but they also have to be prepared to understand the nature and explanation for such discriminatory attitudes and behaviour. It is no longer sufficient to disengage and treat adult service users (particularly white older people) unfavourably because they may hold discriminatory attitudes and behave negatively towards people from a different culture to themselves. Similarly, we would argue that it should not be assumed that adults from minority ethnic backgrounds are automatically supported and provided for by their families. There is still a romanticised idea among many practitioners that all adults from ethnic minority communities, particularly those from Southern Asia, Africa and of Caribbean background, live idyllic lives surrounded by loving and caring family members. However, evidence suggests that in many instances older minority people live isolated lives with a limited social network or support either from their families or their communities. In many cases, because of language barriers and a sense of pride and shame about seeking help, they often live a lonely existence with very little contact with authorities or welfare organisations. There is also evidence, where there are family contacts, that some women from Southern Asia (particular from Pakistan and Bangladesh) face particular difficulties because of cultural and family pressures for them to conform to expectations and not seek outside help or support.

Towards inclusion

The reasons for highlighting these points is not to make life any more difficult for communities or individuals experiencing discrimination but on the contrary it is to encourage an approach that is far more inclusive and moves beyond a simplistic, and increasingly outdated, analysis of culture, identity and social relationships in society. The idea is to move beyond a binary analysis towards one where there is some understanding and acknowledgement that while there are clearly differences between communities and people in society, it is nevertheless just as important to encourage common ground in order to foster a more integrated and, hence, inclusive society. Working with adults in this new framework means not just treating people in a fair and just manner but also recognising (Brofrenbrenner 1979; Thompson 2001) that there is the danger, unwittingly perhaps, of encouraging and indeed promoting a segregated and separatist approach. In essence, a segregated service provision and an essentialist approach (Katz 1996; Gilroy 2000) towards service users are incompatible with our version of Anti-discriminatory practice. In any case, such an approach, we would argue, is against the ethos, spirit and principle of the concept. There is an assumption among many in society that equal opportunity and anti-discriminatory practice relates to and applies to only women and ethnic minorities. Even, for a period at least, some groups who were oppressed, marginalised and discriminated against (lesbians, gay men, people with disability, travellers, older people and white working class) also believed that they were not really included in anti-discriminatory practice. This was somewhat at odds with the reality because from the outset anti-discriminatory practice has embraced all groups and communities. One explanation for the reasons why certain groups or communities may have felt excluded was because some groups and communities had a much higher profile in the debate about discrimination and their experiences were given a greater platform.

DISABILITY

Up until the latter part of the 1990s, the general approach towards disability was governed by a sympathetic and paternalistic attitude. Rather than viewing disability as mere difference and part of a diverse and multifaceted society, people with disability tended to induce in others a combination of fear, embarrassment and uncertainty about how to react. In addition, because social spaces have been constructed in such a way as to benefit the non-disabled, the level of social contact and interaction was limited. The segregation of people with disability starts from the early years; it involves the provision of separate schools, special day centres and residential units for children and adults; and in many cases there was limited access to many of the services and provisions enjoyed and taken for granted by non-disabled people. Of course, the enactment of various legislation (see Chapter 5) has made a difference in the general approach towards disability but equally significant has been the changing attitude towards the whole area of disability. The main goal of many practitioners continues to be how to work in a way that is non-discriminatory and respects the rights and dignity of the service user. There are of course those who maintain that people are impaired but they are disabled by lack of access to the same provisions as non-disabled people (Oliver 1990). For example, the debate about definitions, whether it is disability or impairment and whether the social model is better than the medical model, is unlikely to be resolved soon (Edwards 2005). In our view, anti-discriminatory practice does not mean one excludes or ignores people's disability. In fact, it seems to us a pointless and disingenuous exercise to try and behave as if disability does not exist. For example, as Edwards highlighted, 'disabilities can be physical, intellectual or sensory, and within these broad categories there are extremely wide ranges in degree of severity of a disability' (2005: 52). What is required is not only to see the disability but to see beyond it. As Murphy asserted:

> disability inundated all other claims to social standing, relegating to secondary status all attainments of life, all other social roles, even sexuality. It is not a role, it is an identity, a dominant characteristic to which all social roles must be adjusted. (1987: 90)

This would suggest that anti-discriminatory practice is not just about policies, legal frameworks and structures and systems, although these are an important bulwark against discriminatory practices, but also about people's attitudes and behaviours. It is about the recognition of the complexity of the interaction between people and their social environment. It is also about accepting the fact that people with disability are not one-dimensional but, like everyone else, they have a personality and identity that is borne out of their social, racial and familial background, their sexual orientation and religious beliefs as well as cultural background. According to Bogdan and Taylor (1994) and Vehmas (2008), people's attitudes play a major role in how they view and interact with others. In accepting Bogdan and Taylor's and Vehmas' assertion, it would be of no surprise to suggest that people's views about disability would affect how they relate to and interact with people with disability. Our view is that for anti-discriminatory ideas to remain a pivotal component of practice, it is crucial that a person's identity should not be confined to just one aspect of their make-up but rather all aspects of their identity should be integrated. This is not to ignore the individual's disability or impairment, in fact the contrary is the case – it is to state (the obvious) that the disability is only one aspect of an individual's identity and that there are other aspects that also need to be taken into consideration.

MENTAL HEALTH

For a period in the 1960s and the 1980s, there was a questioning among many practitioners of the very existence of mental illness. The reason for the questioning was largely as a result of the work of Thomas Szasz (1984) and Michel Foucault (198   society that misinterpreted unconventi   rather than the behaviour itself being   d that once an individual is in the mer   into a self-perpetuating cycle. In other   all of their subsequent behaviour is   iental illness. To some extent, there is   iental illness does exist and that it is n

Mental health is one of the m   anyone could experience and the situation is not often helped by negative and discriminatory attitudes towards people who live with the illness. Although there is now a far better understanding of many aspects of the illness and much work has been done to identify predispositions and some of the triggers that cause its onset, there is still a degree of fear surrounding the illness. Although there are some groups who are disproportionately over-represented in the mental health system (young black Afro-Caribbean men, for example), there are some who need help and support but are underrepresented in the system, for example Southern Asian women. One of the greatest strides that has been made in the treatment of mental illness is the development of the social model as a challenge to the medical model. Unlike the medical model with its emphasis on hospitalisation, loss of control and medication, the social model recognises that people are capable of fully participating in society. Treatment is based on agreements between the professionals and the service user. In our view, the dynamic nature of ADP is that, in some instances, hospitalisation is the better option for some service users. In such instances, the best interest of the service user requires a working partnership between the social and medical model. It is our contention that both models should still be governed by the principles and values advocated by ADP.

COMMUNITY DEVELOPMENT

Community development is an important aspect of social welfare provision, although the current approach towards it is somewhat fragmented and unclear. A great deal is said about community cohesion and the need to develop sustainable communities. This notion suggests that society is formed around communities that are easily discernable and that its members know that they are members, that they are able to exercise some influence on it and that they too are influenced by it. In our view, the current approach towards community development is based on the notion that it is through communities that problems, such as anti-social behaviour, violence (muggings, gun and knife attacks) and teenage under-age drinking can be solved. The rationale is that through community pressure individuals would change their behaviour because they would not want to face disapprobation from people around them. There is an unquestioning assumption among politicians, policy makers and some opinion formers that communities not only exist but that they also have a strong influence on their members. Often, individuals are identified as community leaders and a great deal is invested in them and they are expected to act both as the community conscience and as community representative with a mandate to negotiate on behalf of the community. There is an assumption that these individuals represent and speak for the community and that they have power and influence on others within their community. For this line of thinking to make sense, one would have to believe that people are not only part of a community but that they are more likely to respond to its calls.

The segmented and separatist community

There is a tendency to view all minority people as being members of their respective ethnic or cultural communities. Essentially, we would argue that some are seen as citizens of the country while others are seen as members of a community who happen to live in the country. This approach, of viewing people as members of communities rather than as citizens of the country, owes a great deal to the belief that these people are transient and therefore unlikely to settle permanently in the country. However, if they did settle, then they are expected to keep within their own communities. As already discussed, this thinking is based on a particular interpretation of multiculturalism. According to this interpretation, all cultures are equal and efforts should be made to encourage everyone to preserve their language, culture and sense of identity.

While it is not our intention to challenge the existence of different ethnic and cultural communities, we would question the extent to which communities can be viewed in such narrow terms. Although people are from particular communities, their racial and cultural reference point may stretch much wider. So while people may be happy to be identified as part of a particular ethnic and cultural group, that may not be all that identifies them. Also, because they are part of that community, it certainly does not mean they are 'controlled' by the appointed spokespeople of that group. Nor should it be taken for granted that the group necessarily has any influence over their views, attitudes and behaviour. This approach reinforces whatever division already exists in society and it assumes that people owe their allegiance to their respective ethnic and cultural group rather than to the country. This segmented and separatist approach is evident in the over-concentration of particular groups in certain areas of the country. In our view, encouraging cultural, religious and ethnic distinctiveness between groups does very little to support dialogue between disparate groups or promote social cohesion. Community development needs to refocus and decouple itself from a rigid interpretation of how people relate to their community. In other words, people's involvement and commitment to their community should be viewed as transient and fluid. In some cases, the community is the problem rather than the solution and therefore there has to be a mechanism for taking account of the difficulties faced by people that are locked in their community. Also, it is important to understand and accept the limitations of communities. For example, it is unrealistic to believe that communities have the power to prevent crimes, anti-social behaviours or regulate or modify the behaviour of all its members. If only it were so simple and straightforward. Yet there is an unquestioning persistence with the notion of the 'community' being the target for intervention. We would suggest that the target of community development and support should not just be based on cultural, religious, class or racial categorisations but also geographical. It is well recognised that people's social environment and the type of neighbourhood they reside in not only affect their life chances but, we would go further and assert, their outlook and behaviour as well.

CONCLUSION

The early part of the 21st century has seen major population movements both between countries and within countries. Prior to Poland, Romania, Bulgaria and other Eastern European countries joining the European Union and the civil war between Somalia and Eritrea, many of the migrants who came into the country were people mainly from the old and new commonwealth. The situation has changed dramatically and Britain (especially in cities and towns) is truly developing into a multi-racial and multicultural society. Working with different service user groups in this new social landscape requires a deeper level of understanding about difference and diversity. There are new population configurations to consider; for example, unlike the previous migrant population who settled in Britain and whose family are now the 3rd and 4th generations, the new groups have a very different historical relationship to the country. As a result of this population change, anti-discriminatory practice not only has to recognise that the group may face particular difficulty because of their position in society but there may also be a role in educating society about the complexities of living in a multicultural society.

Points to ponder

- Why, despite the enactment of various legislations and a progressive changing social landscape, does there continue to be major concerns about discrimination in society?
- Why is it important that the gains made in developing anti-discriminatory practice should not be underestimated or taken for granted?
- Is it acceptable in a free democratic society for people to face censure because of their language use?
- Should people who have decided to settle in a country be expected to make efforts to integrate into that society or should they be encouraged not to integrate?
- Does the emphasis on community reinforce whatever division already exists in society?
- Should everyone in society be encouraged to owe their allegiance primarily to their respective ethnic and cultural groups rather than to the country?

dynamism of ADP

10
Toward a New Practice Dimension

INTRODUCTION

Experience suggests that it is important for practitioners and the social work profession to maintain their absolute commitment to anti-discriminatory practice. It is evident that the profession has worked very hard in changing from its previous culture of a paternalistic-orientated service to one that genuinely attempts to work in partnership with service users and others. It fosters an inclusive, ethical and non-discriminatory perspective and expects practitioners to be reflective and ground their work, to an extent, in evidence-based practice. A cursory comparison of social work in the 1970s and 1980s with the present would reveal a profession that has done much to confront discriminatory attitudes and behaviours, while at the same time it has done much to improve its practices. We would argue that the profession has not been afraid to acknowledge its mistakes and accept the criticisms that have previously been levelled against it about its discriminatory practices. As we have tried to demonstrate throughout this book, social work and the social work profession faced as much pressure to change from external forces (such as the government, local authorities, agencies, commentators and service users) as it did from within its own ranks.

The struggle of transforming the social work profession has been long and hard and it is therefore important that the gains that have been achieved are protected and embedded within the culture and structure of the profession and further developed in day-to-day practices. It is our contention that there will always be a need to reassert the merits and value of anti-discriminatory practice as each new generation of practitioners enter the profession. The reassertion is important because, despite the entrenchment of anti-discriminatory ideals in legislation and policies, all kinds of discrimination still persist in society. Moreover, and perhaps crucially, the advancement that has been made in challenging discrimination has revealed new challenges that were either previously unforeseen or ignored. For example, the dividing line between the oppressed and the oppressors in this regard is not necessarily as clear-cut as was generally assumed. We have stressed that it is no longer possible to assert that 'all white people are racist', 'all men are sexist', 'all heterosexuals are homophobic', as this would be an over simplification of a complex range of relationships. Similarly, to suggest that being part of a particular social, ethnic, racial, religious group or social class automatically means that one is powerless would be to fall into the trap of determinism and the cul-de-sac of a binary world view. We agree with Thompson's assertion about the impact of discrimination on people's lives in that:

> Existing inequalities are maintained through processes of discrimination that have the effect of allocating life chances, power and resources in such a way as to reinforce existing power relations. It is through this interactive process between discrimination and inequality that the status quo tends to be maintained – with the net result that dominant groups benefit, while the subordinate groups experience a degree of oppression. (2003a: 12)

While it is the case that inequalities are perpetuated through discrimination, the act of discriminating against others is not bound by race, class, gender, disability, sexual orientation or an individual's relation to power. Discrimination operates within and across all of these different boundaries. This is why Thompson's (2003a) 'Personal, Cultural and Structural' schema is such an informative and powerful tool for understanding the different levels at which discrimination operates. Although the personal level highlights the ways prejudices, stereotypical ideas and distorted misinformation about others fuels discrimination, we show below that such behaviour has to be placed in some context. Understanding the context does not imply acceptance of discriminatory attitudes nor does it absolve individuals from taking responsibility for their actions. Rather, it is to acknowledge that cultural and structural considerations also contribute towards the continuation of discrimination. So, while there is a great deal that individuals could do to change their negative and prejudicial attitudes about others, the cultural and structural contexts in which interactions take place also matter greatly. So, as much as people are shaped by the cultures and structures in which they live, the reverse is also true in that people have the ability to contribute to shaping and reshaping the culture and structures around them.

MEANING, IDENTITY AND CULTURE

The argument we have developed is deeply dependent on theoretical debates about meaning, identity, representation and agency. It seeks to understand the functioning of culture in the modern world, how cultural reproduction works and how cultural identities are constructed and organised for individuals and for groups. What determines meaning? Is it the intention, is it the meaning of what is in the text, is it the context (the circumstances or the historical context in which it figures), or is it the experience of the reader? It would be of no surprise to assert that in our view meaning is context bound.

Postmodernism basically states that events occur in the physical world and people give meaning to those events (see Chapter 2). There is no objective meaning and no objective explanation, no objective reality in terms of the explanation of events that occur in the physical world. There are problems with this view as it can suggest that all explanations are simply of equal value. So, critical postmodernism talks about preferred meanings. Whatever position we take flavours our view of the world. Progressive views take the standpoint that race and gender equality is preferable to white male dominance. If there is no objective meaning, then we have to start assessing our values and ethics in relation to these meanings. Issues of values therefore become essential.

Cultures are all about the meanings we give to events. They raise critical issues such as identity and belonging. All cultures carry with them history, beliefs and ways of doing things. For example, people from different cultures have different experiences of migration and of trauma. So within this context, those who are not white are keenly aware that the dominant values from the white group controls all of the institutions in society. The predominance of the values from the white group is experienced as a continuation of the process of colonisation. This can extend to organisational cultures (in the everyday practices of organisations) and, therefore, this can shed light on what happens when people from minority groups, for example black people, work within white organisations.

It cannot be an accident that psychology teaches that belonging and identity are essential for health and human potential. This is why those who are most in need of health and welfare services come disproportionately from cultures that are dominated. This would give professionals a way of understanding why black young men come to be over-represented in prisons and the criminal justice system. In order to aid this understanding, we set the discussion within two domains, namely the domain of identity and the domain of power.

THE DOMAIN OF IDENTITY

The history of the lives of minority groups has been shaped by the ability of powerful others to construct their reality. In Western culture, the construction of identities is thoroughly permeated with the erection of binary oppositions such as white/black, man/woman, good/evil, where the first term is regarded as superior and where the second term contains within it features that pose a threat to the first. Within this discourse, the term black, for example, has been problematised.

Hall (1996) highlights the distinction and the struggle between two models of the production of identities. He articulates the complexity of this debate between modernists and postmodernists by showing that the first model assumes that there is some intrinsic and essential content to any identity, which is defined by either a common origin or a common structure of experience, or by both. Struggling against existing constructions of a particular identity takes the form of contesting negative images with positive ones, and of trying to discover the 'authentic' and 'original' content of the identity. This in essence is the essentialist definition of identity.

The second model emphasises the impossibility of such fully constituted separate and distinct identities. It denies the existence of authentic and original identities based on a universally shared origin or experience. In this model, identities are always relational and incomplete; they are in process. Any identity depends upon its difference from, and its negation of, the former. As Hall puts it, 'Identity is a structured representation which only achieves its positive through the narrow eye of the negative. It has to go through the eye of the needle of the other before it can construct itself' (1991: 12).

Thus, the emphasis is on the multiplicity of identities and differences rather than on a singular identity. The fact of multiple identities gives rise to much more difficult politics, because the sides are neither given in advance, nor in neat divisions. This is indeed very complex. Stuart Hall has spoken of 'Race as a floating signifier'. Others have spoken of race as an 'Empty signifier'. Influenced by Jacques Derrida, such a position sees identity as an entirely cultural, even linguistic construction. However, this presents us with a problem because we have a need to know where to locate ourselves in this. When we use the term black, it is with the tacit knowledge that there are individuals who describe themselves as black and who have an existence that is rooted in reality and they have a connectedness with other people like themselves. So while being clear that race is relational and that identities are changing, complex and contingent, we recognise that some people may need to be strategically essentialist, as suggested by Spivak et al. (1996), in order to be able to invest the term with a particular meaning for the identity of black people.

In thinking about identity, we are recognising its variability. Identity is socially constructed and not innate. It cannot be measured nominally as an objective property of an individual. As Stuart Hall et al. (1992) have emphasised, identity is not stable or fixed but socially and historically constructed and subject to contradictions, revisions and changes. Racism and colonialism, however, are real concepts that impact adversely on groups of people. Pierre Bourdieu's notion of cultural capital is important here. He argues that different social groups possess different sorts of knowledge and skill, they share different cultural histories, and so we would suggest, they experience their contexts differently (Bourdieu 1991). It is more than a truism to say that black and white people bring different perspectives to the same situation.

IDENTITY AS NARRATIVE

The work of Epston and White (1990) highlights how the story that is told about you, in Western culture, and the stories you hear about yourself initiate you into memberships of particular clubs. Some memberships are privileged and elevated while certain memberships are rendered invalid and cast down. Individual identities are shaped and framed by a broader context and in order to reclaim the authorship of stories, it is necessary to deconstruct the stories that are told about minority groups and to understand the nature of the context.

Telling stories is the main way in which we make sense of things. Life follows the logic of the story, where to understand and to make sense is to conceive of how one thing leads to another. There is a basic human drive to hear and tell stories. To tell a story is to claim a certain authority that the author grants. The assumption therefore is that narrative is a fundamental form of knowing; through its sense-making, it gives knowledge of a particular world. To write a story in their own words is to give validity to minority experiences. But as hooks (1995) points out, we are not speaking of replacing one set of absolutes by another, rather it is the experience of learning when one's experience is recognised as central and significant that one is regarded as a subject not an object.

IDENTITY AS PSYCHOLOGICAL DEVELOPMENT

According to object relations theory, along with the earliest development of its sense of separateness, the infant constructs a set of unconscious representations of others in relation to its self, and an internal sense of self-in-relationship emerges (Segal 1988; Anderson 1992; Likierman 2001). As the infant grows and matures, these early images and fragments of perceived experiences become put together into a self. The integration of a 'true self' that feels alive and whole involves a particular set of internalised feelings about others in relation to the self. These feelings all give the self a sense of agency and authenticity (Segal 1988; Anderson 1992; Likierman 2001).

Psychoanalytically, the goals for emotional social life seem to come not only from autonomy and separateness but also from our connectedness with, rather than our separation from, one another. In this sense, identity development takes place within a cultural context. Our sense of differentiation, of separateness from others, as well as our psychological and cultural experience and interpretation of gender and racial difference, is thus created through relational experiences. This leads a way to understanding gender and race differences and human distinctness and separation both relationally and situationally. As we grow up as a self that is, say, a black woman, or a gay man, we enter into and become part of a system of asymmetrical social relationships embedded in inequalities of power, and in which discrimination and oppression take place.

This identification also plays a role in group identities. For members of historically oppressed or marginalised groups, the stories we hear about ourselves prompt identification with a potential group showing us who we are or what we might be. So here is a dilemma: many members of minority groups need to work out the relationship between critiques of essentialist conceptions of identity (of a person or group) and the emotional and political demands to claim an identity. This gives an understanding of why if minorities are to seek liberatory or emancipatory politics, they must adopt identifications of, say, women or black people so that such a politics is possible. For marginalised groups, there are two processes under way. On the one hand, physical traits and characteristics such as skin colour cannot be seen as an essential identity, but on the other hand, black groups may make these imposed identities into resources for that group and a fulcrum around which to organise, fight discrimination and survive. The problem of identity seems unavoidable because of the tensions and conflicts it encapsulates.

Black communities are often critical of education and of educated black people (including black intellectuals) because it is assumed that upwardly mobile educated people will remove themselves from black communities (West 1994). The challenge of black upward mobility results in struggles over leadership and struggles over the definition of who is black and who has the right to define blackness. Hence the name calling that denotes the 'radical' and the 'sell-out'. Authenticity is highly contested. The debate about who is real is seen in discussions of black disengaged youth (Sewell 1997) as well as highly educated university professors (West 1994). It would seem to us that such a demand for authenticity has, at its heart, a notion that black cultures cannot and must not change, and that black people cannot and must not renew and redefine themselves and still remain 'real'. It also stresses that only one axis of identity can be claimed at any one time, i.e. one cannot be black, educated and middle class and remain authentic. Although the example above has focused on ethnicity and black groups in particular, aspects of the analysis are also applicable to other groups we have discussed in this book.

POWER

It is necessary to examine the relationship between knowledge and power and the work of Foucault is one important element in this. Foucault (1980) argues that we are subjected to power through the normalising 'truths' that shape our lives and our relationships. By truths he does not mean that objective or intrinsic facts exist about people but instead the constructed ideas that are accorded a truth status. These truths then construct norms around which people are invited to shape and constitute their lives. When we are subjected to this sort of power through knowledge, we are: 'judged, condemned, classified, determined in our undertaking, destined to a certain mode of living or dying, as a function of the true discourses, which are the bearers of the specific effects of power' (Foucault 1980: 94).

The notion of the discourse is very important in the understanding of power. According to Foucault (1972), discourses are not simply verbal representations or even a way of thinking and producing meaning, they are practices that systematically form the objects of which they speak. This means that they are the beliefs, ideas and practices which come together to organise our relationship with reality. This belief system stresses the particularity of knowledge in that they regulate what is and is not held to be true at a particular moment of time.

The framework of the Enlightenment and its emphasis on representative government sees power as essentially repressive. In opposition to this, Foucault sees power as being dispersed throughout society, it is not possessed by anyone, and it has positive effects. Foucault's conception of the inseparability of power/knowledge is reflected in his challenge to those who would argue that all we need to do is ensure that a different and alternative form of knowledge should take precedence over the others. He would ask, what alternative knowledge would they disqualify, and what persons or group of persons are likely to be diminished through the success of such arguments for ascendancy? According to Derrida (1976), deconstruction involves more than just the reversal of the binary but more a complete strategy that questions fundamentally the very grounds on which the binary has been built.

This means that we need to show a 'passionate commitment to a vision of social transformation rooted in the fundamental belief in a radically democratic idea of freedom and justice for all' (hooks 1995: 26). The challenge for practitioners is to ask whether we can go about our daily professional lives in a way that reflects fully this commitment. In particular, this affects our professional lives in that social work is in constant negotiation with itself and with its wider community and is best understood as a discursive formation.

Anti-discriminatory practice can be seen as the process whereby power is opened up to include new voices and new perspectives so that practice and policy deliberations will be more democratic and less governed by the resources and 'knowledge' of the more powerful. According to Freire (1981), knowledge has been developed and internalised to develop 'cultures of silence' of the oppressed. The issue of silence has been more fully developed in the work of Belenky et al. (1986) in their seminal work *Women's Ways of Knowing*.

Here, countering power involves using knowledge so that people become more aware and conscious of the issues which affect their lives. But we need to go beyond awareness, as people have been aware for a long time. Power can, therefore, be seen as having a more positive attribute. This 'power within' is shaped by one's identity and one's self-concept of agency, not just by outside forces held by the other. Power can be seen as the power to act purposefully in the world. This connects with the notion of empowerment which is so prevalent in social work.

Pierre Bourdieu (1977) stresses that the dominant class does not dominate overtly and does not force the dominated to conform to its will. Nor does it dominate through a conspiracy where the privileged world consciously manipulates reality in accordance with its own self-interest. Rather, the dominant class is, statistically, the beneficiary of economic, social and symbolic power, power which is embodied in economic and cultural capital, and which is located throughout society's institutions and practices and reproduced by these very institutions and practices.

Goldberg (1993) argues that one of the consequences of colonialism is that Western ways of viewing, talking about and interacting are embedded in racialised discourses. Concepts of race intersect with concepts of gender. The process of en-gendering the other has had real consequences for black women in that the ways in which they are described have led to objectification and negative representations. Discriminatory practices are based on the supposed unity of each group which require for their definition and maintenance a sense of exclusion and of otherness. Historically, in the discourse of group oppression, difference is conceived as such otherness and exclusion, and social groups are seen as mutually exclusive and categorically opposed.

In our view, the field of diversity, difference, disadvantage and inequality is littered with binary oppositions. Binary oppositions have one privileged term and the other marginalised, suppressed or excluded. By analysing the second term, Derrida shows that the preference is untenable, as the key term only has meaning by means of its opposition to the other. In other words, it is not pure, it is contaminated by the other.

TRUST

Organisations utilise an excessive amount of energy developing processes and procedures to deal with the consequences of distrust. Procedures are useful instruments to enable people to work effectively in organisations and to protect individuals. But we can get to a stage where the procedures become the end in themselves, long after people have forgotten their original purpose. Decision-making is sometimes so routine that you do not think about it, and it is at these points that the subtle effects of institutional discrimination can be overlooked. According to Schön (1983), reflective practice is about asking why, how and through which human agent. If we do not constantly ask these questions, then we run the risk of dealing only with technical questions rather than moral and ethical ones.

PROBLEMATISING NORMALITY, UNIVERSALITY

The vital question that professionals need to explore when thinking about such matters is 'How did I come to know what I know about the world, about myself and about other people and what do I believe about them?' In this way, social workers are asked to think at a deep level about their taken-for-granted notions of normality, and of its narrow and deeply problematic nature in our society. Hidden within this concept are taken-for-granted notions of gender, race, sexuality, age, disability and religion. We know that social work has meaning but it must also have some way of ultimately explaining and giving meaning to the value of an action by offering a rational choice of that action against competing actions, i.e. social work must be able to maintain its credibility, it must make sense to the people who use its services. Thus, the knowledge base of ADP must claim a paradigm that serves well both the social work profession and its service users. We thus seek to find an epistemology that has at its heart certain key ideas:

- An acknowledgement of diversity, social divisions and conflicts within society, so that the experiences of minority and disadvantaged groups can be understood in a manner that gives them 'voice'.
- That people's experiences cannot be reduced to a set of variables that can be manipulated.
- Reflexivity – where knowledge, values and action are inextricably linked.
- Where a notion of 'critical subjectivity' is given credence, that is, the 'I' of the practitioner is central.
- Where there is no concept of the universal professional or the universal service user.

With this knowledge base, professionals can then ask the key question: how can we build relationships with service users within the context of difference?

Here the notion of the ADP filter is a useful one because this enables us to deal with difference and diversity within the context of the relationship at the earliest stage of the encounter.

It allows professionals and service users to engage with each other while recognising the assumptions that are held about others, understanding the social contexts of people's complex identities and how people promote either trust or mistrust in the light of these differences. If there is no trust then there would need to be a series of precepts or legislation about how people should engage with each other. Anti-discriminatory practice helps us to explore the nature of mistrust and help to bring trust back into the relationship. It must be emphasised that trust is a two-way process and not just about the professional expecting the service user to trust. How do professionals trust service users, service users trust professionals and how do professionals trust their own judgements and other professionals?

Despite the widespread belief that service users are the 'experts' of their own problems (Parker and Bradley 2003), it is often the case that many are unable to articulate their problems or make the necessary connections between what they are currently experiencing and antecedent factors. In other words, it should not be assumed (particularly in this current era of service-user involvement), that all service users are necessarily able to make sense of their situation and condition and therefore able to change it or necessarily offer appropriate solutions. Acknowledging this point does not imply a call to a return to a previous era when service users' voices were ignored and practice was governed by a paternalistic approach, but it is crucial to unashamedly reassert the important role that the practitioner has in the service user–worker relationship. In essence, their role is more than mere conduits or providers of services, as envisaged by the consumerist approach. To be effective, practitioners have to be able to work alongside and guide the service user through the myriad of possibilities and service provisions and act as facilitators of change. As practitioners and 'experts' in the field of human problems and change, they should be guided by theories, models, ideas and approaches that would enable them to do their job effectively and in turn bring about change or at least alleviate people's situation for the better. The social work skill lies in the practitioner's ability to translate these theories, models, ideas and approaches in a way that makes sense and is able to be purposely applied in practice.

In this instance, the practitioner would need to be able to filter service users' stories about their situation and condition through the lens of anti-discriminatory practice (see Figure 10.1). For example, the professional relationship between the practitioner and the service user is not value free nor is it devoid of the inherent tensions that already exist between groups in society. In fact, the tension is further heightened by the unavoidable (but not necessarily negative) power imbalance between the practitioner and the service user. The skill is for the practitioner to understand the nature and extent of their powers; to understand the nature and character of discrimination, including how it operates, its dimension and scope and how it is perpetuated both in organisations and in society. In addition, the practitioner also has to recognise that being a service user is not the sum total of a person's identity. The difficult task for the practitioner is to fuse the knowledge gained about human development and the nature of the range of problems people have with the extent and impact of other considerations such as class, ethnicity, race, gender, impairment, age and sexual orientation on people's life chances and their general place in society. These other aspects overlay whatever is the presenting problem or situation, and are important considerations in all encounters between the practitioner and the service user. Anti-discriminatory practice means taking account of all the different aspects that form the identity of an individual and at the same time connect their situation and experiences to the wider socio-cultural environment in which they live.

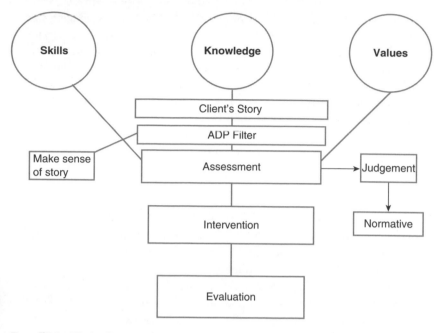

Figure 10.1   Filtering Process

There is the caricature of the doctor who is too busy writing out a prescription before hearing the patient's story to find out what was wrong. In the same way, social workers are deemed to be too busy filling out forms to listen to service users' stories. So if ADP represents the quality of listening to the service user's story and the quality of seeing the service user in all aspects of her/his identity, we need to look at identities and power in a more complex manner.

Wilson and Beresford (2000) question the knowledge of anti-oppressive practice because none of it was delivered or written by service users. This is interesting because it speaks to the nature of power/knowledge and to the voice of the service user. However, in much of the discourse about service-user participation and involvement, there has often been an uncritical acceptance of the service-user identity as a fixed identity, which is itself an essentialist notion of identity. Furthermore, it demonstrates lack of trust in a practitioner's ability to develop ideas and concepts (without the involvement of service users) that are motivated by compassion, justice and fairness and are in the best interest of service users.

THE PARADOX OF TOLERANCE

There is a belief, based on lack of clarity, about the concept and perhaps fear that anti-discriminatory ideas and their underlying principles are absolute concepts. Furthermore, there is collective amnesia as to the primary and general concerns of anti-discriminatory practice. As we have already explored in some detail, the whole purpose was to create a society that is tolerant and non-discriminatory, one that champions economic, social and political justice and enables equality of opportunity for all. There is also an expectation of religious tolerance and, where possible and within the law, the accommodation of difference. On the face of it, it seems clear, however, that tolerance and recognising difference does not mean that society and organisations should stop functioning in order to accommodate cultural idiosyncrasies. In this regard, anti-discriminatory practice means finding ways to accommodate difference but also recognising that in some instances it is not about exercising one's right but in fact working out a solution in situations that may only affect particular groups of people.

In this respect, anti-discriminatory practice is in accord with Article 9 of the European Convention on Human Rights. Specifically, Article 9 states:

> Everyone has the right to freedom of thought, conscience and religion; this right includes freedom to change his religion or belief and freedom, either alone or in community with others and in public or private, to manifest his religion or belief, in worship, teaching, practice and observance. (1989)

Sensibly, of course, this is not an absolute right because as the proviso contained in Article 9 makes clear:

> Freedom to manifest one's religion or beliefs shall be subject only to such limitations as are prescribed by law and are necessary in a democratic society in the interests of public safety, for the protection of public order, health or morals, or for the protection of the rights and freedoms of others. (1989)

The danger of misunderstanding and misinterpretation of anti-discriminatory practice is that it alienates people, causes resentment and damages the credibility of the concept. While some may argue that this may be a price worth paying in order to ensure that everyone's needs, irrespective of what they are, are met, we would caution against such a strident and unqualified view. It is worth remembering that in a democracy where people are able to exercise their 'rights' through the electoral system, the irony is that we may end up with the worst of both worlds starting with the repeal of ECHR and the eventual dismantling of the anti-discriminatory practice structures that have taken so long to build.

A MODERNIST RESPONSE IN A DIFFERENT AGE

Anti-discriminatory practice was forged from the ideological discourse of the modernist era. Effectively, anti-discriminatory approaches, policies and legislation were developed to have a universal application that transcends individuals and groups. It does not distinguish between people nor does it valorise one group above others, rather it calls for an even-handed approach because it recognises the subjective and idiosyncratic nature of discrimination. The difficulty for Anti-discriminatory practice (as discussed in Chapters 2 and 3) is that it has had to maintain a constant and universalistic perspective despite attempts to particularise it. In addition, it has to remain relevant to disparate groups who not merely hold different views, perspectives and beliefs but are fundamentally opposed to each other. The attempt to particularise anti-discriminatory practice and relegate it to a relativistic personal-cultural doctrine is very postmodern. However, we must continue to recognise the universal nature of the concept so as not to misunderstand its principle as well as its aims and objectives, thus diminishing its capacity and function and relegating it to the margins of social work practice. The point of tension for many people is how could anti-discriminatory practice face different directions at the same time? We ask the question because the concept encourages and demands tolerance, understanding and open-mindedness towards those who have been identified as oppressors, and at the same time it requires those who see themselves as oppressed to also change their dearly held values and beliefs which may be deemed discriminatory by others. For example, is it right to demand that a practitioner goes against their cultural values and their religious beliefs because it is incompatible with a way of working that adheres to anti-discriminatory principles? Could the same practitioner demand that people respect and not discriminate against them because of their cultural practices and religious beliefs even though others may find these both offensive and discriminatory?

The point being made is that the approaches taken towards Anti-discriminatory practice have tended to encourage treating different areas of discrimination as discrete entities without necessarily cross-referencing to other areas of discrimination. Similarly, practice approaches are generally dominated by the assumption that each area of discrimination is unique and, therefore, needs to be explored separately. While the underlying principle for taking this kind of sectarian approach is understandable, it is this type of thinking, however, that has sometimes rendered practitioners powerless in the face of situations that warrant decisive, and perhaps draconian, action. It could be argued that the current approach tends to view people in segmented forms and they are addressed as if they possess only one identity and that identity informs all that needs to be known about them.

REENERGISING ADP

There is no doubt that there is a greater emphasis on the European Convention on Human Rights as a means of challenging discrimination and unfair treatment. Increasingly, individuals and groups are looking to the Act to challenge discriminatory practices and to gain redress from organisations or their employers. Although some people now take a more litigious approach to dealing with their experiences of unfairness and discrimination, we still believe, however, certainly as far as social work and social welfare are concerned, that practitioners should continue to view anti-discriminatory practice as an important approach in the way they confront and tackle all forms of discriminations and discriminatory practices. One of the main reasons why practitioners maintain their commitment to anti-discriminatory practice is that despite the increasing reliance on the legal framework, the first recognition of discrimination is the contact and interaction between people. It is within this encounter that prejudices, unfairness and discriminatory values, attitudes and behaviours are initially played out.

So while there is a place for litigation and seeking redress using appropriate legal frameworks, there is still a need to further embed Anti-discriminatory practice in the structures, systems and processes of (all) social work and social welfare organisations. Similarly, how practitioners approach their work, in terms of their attitudes, professionalism, beliefs and values is of great importance to both service users and others. We would not like to give the impression that service users are wretched and helpless victims who need the good will and benevolence of the practitioner. However, the practitioner does need to be constantly aware of their role, duties and responsibilities and the power they hold in relation to the service user. It is during their encounters, however brief, with service users and others that discriminatory practices comes to the fore. There are many signifiers such as language used, including tonality, body language, expressions, dress code and attitudes that contribute towards the impression that the practitioner creates about their 'feelings' towards the service user. It is this interaction of different identities, different cultures and different meanings and the judicious exercise of power that means that anti-discriminatory practice continues to be a key concept in social work and social care practice. Of course, it may be the case that the positive and anti-discriminatory impressions that the practitioner tries to convey are not correctly interpreted by the service user, but the important point is that the practitioner has a sharpened sense of awareness about the value-laden nature of their encounters with service users.

TOWARDS A NEW PRACTICE DIMENSION

Social workers practice within a framework of standards and key roles that cover all areas of their work. These areas of practice include assessing and working with people and communities; planning, intervening, reviewing and evaluating practice; supporting and representing service users' views and circumstances; managing risks; managing and being accountable (with supervision and support) for own practice; and demonstrating competence in practice. These areas, together with the occupational standards, are the cornerstones of practice and they clearly set out the expectations, requirements and responsibilities of practitioners. But as well as these skills and roles, practitioners should of course be practising within a professional knowledge base and their practice should be informed by social work values and ethical considerations that are set out in Codes of Practice. Higham (2006) also acknowledges the range out professional roles that are performed by social workers and suggests that they need to be flexible and versatile in the way they apply these roles. Higham believes the key roles include:

- planner
- assessor
- evaluator
- counsellor
- supporter
- advocate
- manager.

She makes the point that 'Social workers demonstrate their professionalism by combining roles appropriately within service user situations and professional environments. Social workers need more than "one string to their bow". They have to combine roles for effective practice' (Higham 2006: 84). In addition to those identified by Higham, we would add other crucial aspects of the social work role which are often ignored. These would include being an enabler, facilitator, educator and mentor.

It is evident that the social work profession will continue to evolve as do the demands placed on it and its priorities. Unfortunately, the profession is subject to close scrutiny because of the lack of trust in its ability to prevent harm or death. There is an expectation that social work should have the ability to identify service users who are at risk and to be proactive in intervening earlier in order to prevent neglect, abuse and fatal tragedies. The new externally driven practice dimension, implicitly, calls on social workers to be more decisive in identifying individuals in order to anticipate events and prevent negative outcomes. Although the profession agrees about the need to be proactive and preventative, it tries not to pathologise individuals and groups and still believes in the ability of service users to transform their lives given the appropriate level of help and support. Practitioners are aware that some problems are caused by or arise because of social and economic reasons and are not intrinsic to the person, even if they most definitely should be the subject of social work concern. The same observation was made by Ferguson who said:

> In contrast to theories of society which locate the roots of social problems *within* the individual, most social work theories, including most mainstream theories, have tended to emphasise the interaction *between* the individual and society (or environment). To that extent social work challenges explanations of social problems which seek to reduce them to the behaviours of individuals. (2008: 19)

Although there is a changing practice landscape, the tenets of and justification for anti-discriminatory practice remain constant. Just as practitioners recognise that not all problems can be attributed to an individual's personal failings, similarly the reasons for and the causes of discrimination cannot be understood merely by a uni-causal explanation. Anti-discriminatory practice was founded on very sound principles from a combination of ideas borrowed from philosophy, politics and religion. While it may be argued that it was the radical politics of the 1960s and 1970s that gave anti-discriminatory practice its current shape, we have shown that the underlying ideas and its core elements have a longer history.

People experience discrimination at different levels and in different forms. The complexity of the nature and experience of discrimination makes it important that practitioners view people's experiences through a holistic lens. People are neither static beings nor are they mere puppets under the control of the social environment in which they live. It is our contention that the National Occupational Standards, Key Roles and the professional standards and Code of Conduct all recognise the dynamic and fluidity of people's existence, hence the need for a reflective and reflexive approach. Similarly, anti-discriminatory practice demands an approach that views people as complex beings, whose identity, culture and social relationships are not necessarily predetermined or fixed. Of course, there would be those who take a contrary viewpoint, however our contention is that in order for the anti-discriminatory approach not to replicate or reinforce discriminations in society, it has to be able to withstand criticisms and challenge the deterministic views about people in society. In a democratic, liberal, welfare state such as Britain, it is difficult to maintain the view that all areas of people's existence are necessarily predetermined or fixed indefinitely.

INTEGRATION OF THE SELF

As we have consistently maintained throughout this book, it would be simply illogical to view people's experiences in isolation of other considerations. Similarly, while we are all products of history, we should not be constrained or paralysed by it. Instead, history should be viewed as a means of understanding the present and perhaps as a warning about the future. In order for anti-discriminatory practice to still remain relevant, it has to be able to take account of individual experiences while ensuring that its main purpose is not compromised. Practitioners should see anti-discriminatory practice as a means of developing meaningful engagement with service users. Similar to the ecological model, anti-discriminatory practice must take account of all areas of service users' reality. In other words, rather than viewing someone as just a service user, with all the implied connotation and assumptions, all other aspects of the person should be taken into account as a means of understanding the person's situation and condition. Striving to develop a better understanding of the service user's condition and situation should not be read to mean the encouragement of an unreasonable over-identification with the service user. Understanding people's situation and working within the framework of anti-discriminatory practice should not mean that practitioners are forced into inaction or induce powerlessness because they fear that they might appear to be oppressive or discriminatory. It is important to clearly state that the roles, duties and responsibilities of social work practitioners and their statutory powers are not in themselves problematic nor are they inherently discriminatory. The concerns are about how these requirements and expectations are applied in practice.

CONCLUSION

The emphasis throughout this publication has been to encourage practitioners to be less defensive in their approach and to foster the necessary confidence to challenge (in a constructive and empowering way) discriminatory practices. It is clear that changes in legislation have continued to impact on practitioners' and organisations' attitudes and behaviour towards anti-discriminatory practice. Although a relatively recent phenomenon, many organisations (it is a requirement for statutory organisations) evaluate and continually monitor the level of diversity within their organisations. Those organisations that are fully committed to anti-discriminatory practice do not only monitor how the policy is working but they actively seek ways to improve both the diversity and practices of their workforce. Organisations convey their key messages about equal opportunities in a variety of forms, so that both the public and their staff are aware of their commitment and their intent to provide services that are free of bias and discrimination. Practitioners are acutely aware of the continual changes that are taking place in social work practice. The changes include greater demand for scarce resources, increased complexity of the role and the workload, and more diverse service user groups. In this challenging environment, practitioners need to maintain and develop both a general understanding of the underlying issues that affect people and think about the application of anti-discriminatory practice. Finally, it is important that Anti-discriminatory practice continues to be re-evaluated and reconsidered in terms of its purpose, function and focus. Such renewal and reenergising would result in the concept becoming more coherent and applicable and therefore more relevant in a continually changing social and practice landscape.

bibliography

Adams, John (1995) *Risk*. London: Routledge.

Adams, Robert, Dominelli, Lena and Payne, Malcolm (2002) (eds) *Critical Practice in Social Work*. Basingstoke: Palgrave.

Ahmed, Shah, Cheetham, Juliet and Small, John (1986) (eds) *Social Work with Black Children and their Families*. London: Batsford.

Ainsworth, Mary, Blehar, Mary C., Waters, Everett and Wall, Sally (1978) *Patterns of Attachment: A Psychological Study of the Strange Situation*. New Jersey: Erlbaum.

Anderson, James A. (1992) *Communication Yearbook* (Vol. 14, pp. 256–287). Newbury, CA: Sage.

Article 19 Pamphlet, The International Committee for the Defence of Salman Rushdie and his Publishers. London: ICDSR Publications.

Assiter, Alison (1984) 'Althusser and Structuralism', *The British Journal of Sociology*, 35(2): 272–296.

Bagley, Christopher and Young, Loretta (1982) Policy Dilemmas and the Adoption of Black Children. In Cheetham, Juliet (ed.) *Social Work and Ethnicity*. London: Allen and Unwin.

Bailey, Roy and Brake, Mike (1975) *Radical Social Work*. London: Edward Arnold.

Banks, Sara (2001) *Ethics and Values in Social Work*. Basingstoke: Palgrave/Macmillan.

Banyard, Kat (2008) quoted in Carvel, John (2008) TUC Attacks Motherhood Penalty in the Workplace, *Guardian*, 11 March.

Barn, Ravinder (1993) *Black Children in the Public Care System*. London: Batsford.

Barnes, Colin and Mercer, Geoff (2003) *Disability: Key Concepts*. Cambridge: Polity.

Banton, Michael (1984) *Race Relations*. London: Tavistock.

BASW (British Association of Social Workers) (2001) *The Code of Ethics for Social Work*. Birmingham: BASW Publications.

Beckett, Chris and Maynard, Andrew (2005) *Values and Ethics in Social Work: An Introduction*. London: Sage.

Belenky, Mary, Clinchy, Blythe, Goldberger, Nancy and Tarule, Jill (1986) *Women's Ways of Knowing: The Development of Self, Voice and Mind*. New York: Basic Books.

Biestek, Felix Paul (1961) *Case Work Relationship*. London: Allen and Unwin.

Blom-Cooper, (1985) A Child in Trust. Inquiry into the circumstances surrounding the death of Jasmine Beckford. Wembley: London Borough of Brent.

Bogdan, Robert and Taylor, Steven J. (1994) *The Social Meaning of Mental Retardation: Two Life Stories*. New York: Teachers College Press.

Bourdieu, Pierre (1977) 'Reproduction in Education', *Society and Culture*. London: Sage.

Bourdieu, Pierre (1991) *Language and Smbolic Power*. Cambridge: Polity

Bowlby, John (1951) 'Maternal Care and Mental Health', *World Health Organization Monograph* (Serial No. 2).

Braye, Suzie and Preston-Shoot, Michael (1998) *Practising Social Work Law*. Buckingham: Open University Press.

bibliography

161

Brayne, Hugh and Carr, Helen (2005) *Law for Social Workers*. 9th edition. Oxford: Oxford University Press.

Brockes, Emma (2001) It's a Man's World, *Guardian*, 19 March.

Brofrenbrenner, Uri (1979) *The Ecology of Human Development*. Cambridge, MA: Havard University Press.

Brown, Helen Cosis (1992) Lesbians, the State and Social Work Practice. In Langan, Mary and Day, Lesley (eds), *Women, Oppression and Social Work: Issues in Anti-discriminatory Practice*. London: Routledge. pp. 201–219.

Caplan, Gerald (1964) *Principles of Preventative Psychiatry*. London: Tavistock Publications.

Carvel, John (2008) TUC Attacks Motherhood Penalty in the Workplace, *Guardian*, 11 March.

Case Con Manifesto (1970) *The Case Con Manifesto*. London: Case Con Group.

Clarke, Kris (1999) *Breaking the Bounds of Bifurcation: The Challenge of Multiculturalism in Finnish Vocational Social Education*. Tampere: Tampere University Press.

Cohen, Nick (2008) Comment: Charles, a very Modern Marie Antoinette, *The Observer*, 17 August.

Commission for Equality and Human Rights (2008) *Role of the Commission for Equality and Human Rights*. London, HMSO.

Corden, John and Preston-Shoot, Michael (1987) *Contracts in Social Work*. Aldershot: Gower.

Coulshed, Veronica (1988) *Social Work Practice: An Introduction*. Basingstoke: Macmillan.

Coulshed, Veronica and Orme, Joan (2006) *Social Work Practice*. 4th edition. London: British Association of Social Workers.

Cranston, Maurice (1968) *Jean-Jacques Rousseau. A Discourse on Inequality*. Harmondsworth: Penguin.

Crawford, Karin and Walker, Janet (2004) *Social Work with Older People*. Exeter: Learning Matters.

Crisp, Beth R., Anderson, Mark R., Orme, Joan and Lister, Pam (2003) *SCIE Knowledge Review I*. SCIE Publications.

Dawkins Richard (2006) *The God Delusion*. London: Transworld Publications.

Derrida, Jacques (1976) *Of Grammatology*. Baltimore: Johns Hopkins.

Dominelli, Lena (1988) *Anti-Racist Social Work. A Challenge for White Practitioners and Educators*. Basingstoke: MacMillan.

Dominelli, Lena (1993) *Social Work: Mirror of Society or its Conscience?* Sheffield: University of Sheffield, Department of Sociological Studies.

Dominelli, Lena (2002) *Anti-oppressive Practice*. Basingstoke: Palgrave.

Dominelli, Lena (2004) *Social Work. Theory Practice for a Changing Profession*. Cambridge: Polity.

Edwards, Steven (2005) *Disability: Definitions, Value and Identity*. Oxford: Radcliffe Publishing.

Epston, David and White, Michael (1990) *Narrative Means to Therapeutic Ends*. New York: Norton.

Erikson, Erik (1965) *Identity and the Life Cycle*. New York: Norton Press.

European Convention on Human Rights (1998).

Ferguson, Iain (2008) *Reclaiming Social Work: Challenging Neo-Liberalism and Promoting Social Justice*. London: Sage.

Forsythe, Bill (1995) 'Discrimination in Social Work: An Historical Note', *British Journal of Social Work*, 25: 1–16.

Foucault, Michel (1972) *The Archaeology of Knowledge*. London: Tavistock Publications.

Foucault, Michel (1976) Society Must Be Defended: Lectures at the Collège de France, 1975–76, Lecture series (7 January). London: Penguin Books.

Foucault, Michel (1980) *Power/Knowledge: Selected Interviews and Other Writings, 1972–1977*. New York: Pantheon.

Foucault, Michel (1984) *The Foucault Reader: An Introduction to Foucault's Thought*. London: Penquin.

Freire, Paulo (1981) *Pedogogy of the Oppressed*. New York: Continum.

Fryer, Peter (1984) *Staying Power*. London: Pluto.

Giddens, Anthony (1989) *Sociology*. Cambridge: Polity Press.

Giddens, Anthony (2002) *The Third Way: The Renewal of Social Democracy*. Cambridge: Polity Press.

Gilroy, Paul (1987) *There Ain't no Black in the Union Jack*. London: Unwin Hyman Ltd.

Gilroy, Paul (2000) *Between Camps: Nations, Cultures and Allure of Race*. London: Penguin Press.

Goodyer, Annabel (2008) Assessment in Practice. In Okitikpi, Toyin and Aymer, Cathy (eds) *The Art of Social Work Practice*. Lyme Regis: Russell House Publishing. pp. 1–12.

Goffman, Erving (1971) *Relations in Public: Microstudies of the Public Order*. London: Allen Lane.

Goldberg, David Theo (1993) *Racist Culture: Philosophy and the Politics of Meaning*. Cambridge, MA: Blackwell.

Hall, Stuart (1996) *Critical Dialogues in Cultural Studies*. London: Routledge.

Hall, Stuart (1991) 'Ethnicity, Identity and Difference', *Radical America*, 23(4): 9–20.

Hall, Stuart et al. (1992) *Modernity and its Futures*. Cambridge: Polity Press in association with the Open University.

Handy, Charles (2005) *Understanding Organisations*. 4th edition. London: Penguin.

Heywood, Andrew (2007) *Political Ideology: An Introduction*. 4th edition. Basingstoke: Palgrave/Macmillan.

Higham, Patricia (2006) *Social Work: Introducing Professional Practice*. London: Sage.

Hollis, Florence and Woods, Mary (1981) *Case Work: A Psychosocial Therapy*. New York: McGraw-Hill Education.

hooks, bell (1995) *Killing Rage: Ending Racism*. London: Penguin.

Horner, Nigel (2003) *What is Social Work? Contexts and Perspectives*. Exeter: Learning Matters.

International Federation of Social Workers/International Association of Schools of Social Work (2003) *Codes of Ethics*. New York: IFSW/IASSW.

Jahoda, Gustav (1999) *Images of Savages. Ancient Roots of Modern Prejudices in Western Culture*. London: Routledge.

Kai, Joe (ed.) (2003) *Ethnicity, Health and Primary Care*. Oxford: Oxford Medical Press.

Kashima, Yoshihisa, Fiedler, Klaus and Freytag, Peter (eds) (2008) *Stereotype Dynamics: Language-Based Approach to the Formation, Maintenance, and Transformation of Stereotypes*. New York: Lawrence Erlbaum.

Katz, Ilan (1996) *The Construction of Racial Identity in Children of Mixed Parentage: Mixed Metaphor*. London: Jessica Kingsley Publications.

Katz, Judy H. (1978) *White Awareness: Handbook for Anti-Racism Training*. Norman: University of Oklahoma Press.

Klein, Melanie (1984) *Envy and Gratitude and Other Works, 1946–1963*. London: The Free Press.

Lacan, Jacques (2008) *My Teaching*. London: Verso Books.

Langan, Mary and Day, Lesley (eds) (1992) *Women Oppression and Social Work: Issues in Anti-discriminatory Practice*. London: Routledge.

Lavalette, Michael and Penketh, Laura (2006) Forward Thinking, *Guardian – Society*, 22 March.

Lechte, John (1994) *Fifty Key Contemporary Thinkers: From Structuralism to Postmodernity*. London: Routledge.

Likierman, Meira (2001) *Melanie Klein: Her Work in Context*. London and New York: Continuum.

Lymbery Mark and Butler, Sandra (eds) (2004) *Social Work: Ideas and Practice Realities*. Basingstoke: Palgrave/Macmillan.

Macpherson, William (1999) *An Inquiry into the Death of Stephen Lawrence*. London: HMSO.

Medcof, John and Roth, John (eds) (1979) *Approaches to Psychology*. Milton Keynes: Open University Press.

Middleton, Laura (1997) *The Art of Assessment*. Birmingham: Venture Press.

Miles, Robert (1990) *Racism*. London: Routledge.

Miller, Cynthia L. (1987) 'Qualitative Differences Amongst Gender Stereotyped Toys: The Implication for Cognitive and Social Development in Girls and Boys', *Sex Roles*, 16: 473–487.

Millam, Rosalind (2002) *Anti-discriminatory Practice: A Guide for Workers in Childcare and Education*. 2nd edition. London: Continuum.

Milner, David (1993) *Children and Race: Ten Years On*. London: Ward Lock.

Moonie, Neil, Bates, Ann and Spencer-Perkins, Dee (2004) *Diversity and Rights in Care*. Oxford: Heinmann.

Murphy, Robert (1987) *The Body Silent*. London: Dent.

National Research Council (USA) (1983) *Risk Assessment*. Washington, DC: National Academy Press.

Office of Public Sector Information (2008) *Information Fact Sheet*. London, HMSO.

Okitikpi, Toyin (2004) Anti-Discriminatory and Anti-Oppressive Practice: Working with Ethnic Minority Children in Foster and Residential Care. In Eriksson, Hans Goran and Tjelflaat, Torill (eds) *Residential Care: Horizons for the New Century*. Aldershot: Ashgate. pp.130–142.

Okitikpi, Toyin (2005) (ed.) *Working with Children of Mixed Parentage*. Lyme Regis: Russell House Publishing.

Okitikpi, Toyin and Aymer, Cathy (eds) (2008) *The Art of Social Work Practice*. Lyme Regis: Russell House Publishing.

Oliver, Michael (1990) *The Politics of Disablement*. London: Macmillan.

Parker, Jonathan and Bradley, Greta (2003) *Social Work Practice: Assessment, Planning, Intervention and Review*. Exeter: Learning Matters.

Patni, Rachana (2008) Communication in Social Work. In Okitikpi, Toyin and Aymer, Cathy (eds) *The Art of Social Work Practice*. Lyme Regis: Russell House Publishing. pp. 71–85.

Payne, Malcolm (1997) *Social Work Theory*. 2nd edition. London: Macmillan.

Payne, Malcolm (2005) *Modern Social Work Theory*. 3rd edition. Basingstoke: Palgrave-Macmillan.

Pinker, Robert (1979) *The Idea of Welfare*. London: Heinemann.

Pinker, Steven (2002) *The Blank Slate*. London: Penguin.

Pitts, John (2008) Private conversation about discriminatory practices within the welfare state.

Plant, Raymond, Lesser, Harry and Taylor-Gooby, Peter (1980) *Political Philosophy and Social Welfare. Essays on the Normative Basis of Welfare Provision*. London: Routledge, Kegan and Paul.

Preston-Shoot, Michael (2008) Private conversation about discriminatory practices within the welfare state.

Rapoport, Lydia (1970) Crisis Intervention as a Brief Mode of Treatment. In Roberts, Robert and Nee, Robert (eds) *Theories of Social Casework*. Chicago: University of Chicago Press.

Rees, Stuart (1991) *Achieving Power: Practice and Policy in Social Welfare*. Sydney: Allen and Unwin.

Reid, William and Epstein, Laura (1972) *Task Centred Casework*. Columbia: Columbia University Press.

Rex, John (1970) *Race Relations in Sociological Theory*. London: Weidenfeld and Nicolson.

Roberts, Celia, Davies, Evelyn and Jupp, Tom (1992) *Language and Discrimination: A Study of Communication in Multi-ethnic Workplaces*. London: Longman.

Rogers, Carl (1951) *Client Centred Therapy: Its Current Practice, Implication and Theory*. London: Constable.

Rogers, Carl (1961) *On Becoming a Person: A Therapist's View of Psychotherapy*. London: Constable.

Rojek, Chris, Peacock, Geraldine and Collins, Stewart (1988) *Social Work and Received Ideas*. London: Routledge.

Rushdie, Salman (1988) *The Satanic Verses*. London: Viking.

Sarup, Madan (1993) *An Introductory Guide to Post-Structuralism and Post Modernism 2nd edition*. New York: Harvester/Wheatsheaf.

Schoenberg, Robert, Goldberg, Richard S. and Shore, David (eds) (1985) Homosexuality and Social Work. *Journal of Social Work and Human Sexuality*, 2 (2/3).

Segal, Hanna (1988) *Introduction to the work of Melanie Klein*. London: Karnac Books.

Sewell, Tony (1997) *Black masculinities and schooling: how Black boys survive modern schooling*. Stoke on Trent, UK: Trentham Books.

Schön, Donald (1983) *The Reflective Practitioner*. New York: Basic Books.

Schön, Donald (1987) *Educating the Reflective Practitioner*. Jossey-Bass: San Francisco.

Shardlow, Steven (2002) *Social Work Values and Knowledge*. Basingstoke: Palgrave Macmillan.

Sivanandan, Ambalavaner (1990) *Communities of Resistance: Writings on Black Struggles for Socialism*. London: Verso.

Smalley, Ruth (1970) The Functionalist Approach to Case Work Practice. In Roberts, Robert and Nee, Robert (eds) *Theories of Social Casework*. Chicago: University of Chicago Press.

Somerville, Peter and Steele, Andy (2002) *Race, Housing and Social Exclusion*. London: Jessica Kingsley Publishers.

Spivak, Gayatri, Landry, Donna and Maclean, Gerald (1996). *The Spivak Reader: Selected Works of Gayatri Chakravorty Spivak*. New York: Routledge.

Spender, Dale (1990) *Man Made Language*. 2nd edition. Basingstoke: Macmillan.

Szasz, S. Thomas (1984) *The Myth of Mental Illness: The Foundation of a Theory of Personal Contact*. Chicago: Chicago Press.

Tannen, Deborah (1995) *You Just Don't Understand. Men and Women in Conversation*. London: Virago Press.

Temkin, Jennifer and Krahe, Barbara (2008) *Sexual Assault and the Justice Gap*. London: Hart Publishing.

The Law Commission (1985) *Offences Against Religion and Public Worship*. Law Commission Report Number 145. London: Her Majesty's Stationery Office.

Thompson, Neil (2000) *Theory and Practice in Human Services*. 2nd edition. Buckingham: Open University Press.

Thompson, Neil (2003a) *Promoting Equality: Challenging Discrimination and Oppression*. 2nd edition. Basingstoke: Palgrave.

Thompson, Neil (2003b) *Communication and Language. A Handbook of Theory and Practice*. Basingstoke: Palgrave/Macmillan.

Thompson, Neil (2005) *Understanding Social Work: Preparing for Practice*. Basingstoke: Palgrave Macmillan.

Thompson, Neil (2006) *Anti-Discriminatory Practice*. 4th edition. Basingstoke: Palgrave/Macmillan.

Titmus, Richard (1976) *Essays on the Welfare State*. 3rd edition. London: Allen and Unwin.

Trevithick, Pamela (2000) *Social Work Skills. Practice Handbook*. Buckingham: Open University Press.

Vehmas, Simo (2008) Ethical Analysis of the Concept of Disability. In Watson, Nick (ed.) *Disability: Major Themes in Health and Social Welfare*. London: Routledge. pp. 209–222.

Vivian, James and Brown, Rupert (1995) Prejudice and Intergroup Conflict. In Argyle, Michael and Coleman, Andrew (eds) *Social Psychology*. London: Longman.

Vygotsky, Lev (1986) *Thought and Language*. Cambridge, MA: MIT Press.

Waddington, Kevin (1974) *Outlines of Marxist Philosophy*. London: Lawrence and Wishart.

Watson, David and West, Janice (2006) *Social Work Process and Practice: Approaches, Knowledge and Skills*. Basingstoke: Palgrave/Macmillan.

West, Cornel (ed.) (1994) *Race Matters*. New York: Vintage Books.

Williams, Fiona (1992) Women with Learning Difficulties are Women Too. In Langan, Mary and Day, Lesley (eds) *Women, Oppression and Social Work: Issues in Anti-discriminatory Practice*. London: Routledge.

Wilson, Anne and Beresford, Peter (2000) 'Anti-oppressive Practice: Emancipation or Appropriation?', *British Journal of Social Work*, 30(5): 553–573.

key concepts in anti-discriminatory social work

index

index